Above and Below:
Silent Heroes of World War II

The Close Encounter of an American Sailor
and a German U-Boat Commander

Lee Bryan

Edited by Charlie McKee, Editor's Proof

Cover design by Sharon K. Miller, Buckskin Books LLC

Indexed by Nan Badgett, dba Wordability

Cover photos: (top right) Ernest Bryan, courtesy of Bryan Family Collection; (bottom left) Wilhelm Franken, https://uboat.net; (top left) Esso Montpelier in rough seas. courtesy Auke Visser; (bottom right) German U-boat submarine, public domain; and (background) U-boat 565 War Journal sketch, April 20, 1943, by KptLt. Wilhelm Franken, National Archives and Records Administration, College Park, Maryland.

ISBN (hardback): 978-1-7358480-2-0
ISBN (paperback): 978-1-7358480-0-6
ISBN (e-book): 978-1-7358480-1-3

 WW2 Publishing
P.O. Box 20232
Sedona, AZ 86341
www.WW2Publishing.com
LBryan.ww2@gmail.com

*Dedicated to the men
who fought in the Battle of the Atlantic
and to the memories of those who are now gone.*

TABLE OF CONTENTS

Acknowledgements   vii

Preface   xi

Prologue   1

CHAPTER ONE   America Enters World War II   5

CHAPTER TWO   Ten Years Earlier in Florida   19

CHAPTER THREE   Ready to Serve His Country   25

CHAPTER FOUR   Convoy UGS-4: SS *Esso Montpelier*   35

CHAPTER FIVE   Early Years: Wilhelm Franken in Germany and at War   47

CHAPTER SIX   Evasive Measures…Crash Dive   55

CHAPTER SEVEN   Times of Courage   69

CHAPTER EIGHT   Convoy UGS-7 Underway   77

CHAPTER NINE   The Stalking of Convoy UGS-7   89

CHAPTER TEN   Delivering the Vital Cargo   103

CHAPTER ELEVEN   Homeward Bound   111

CHAPTER TWELVE   The Defeat of the U-Boat   121

CHAPTER THIRTEEN   The Tragic Loss of a Hero   131

CHAPTER FOURTEEN   War Comes to an End   141

Epilogue   153

APPENDIX I   SS *Esso Montpelier* Oil Tanker   161

APPENDIX II   *U-565* War Diary Comments by the FdU and the BdU   167

APPENDIX III   UGS-7 Convoy Fleet List   171

APPENDIX IV   Translated War Diary Patrol Report of KptLt. Franken   177

APPENDIX V   Handwritten Journal of Armed Guard S/1C Ernest Bryan   187

APPENDIX VI   HX-242 Convoy Fleet List   191

Appendix VII   Comments of the FdU Italien on the War Diary of *U-565*   199

Appendix VIII   North Atlantic and Mid-Atlantic Convoy Routing   203

Glossary of Navy Terms   205

Bibliography   211

Credits: Illustrations, Photographs, Charts, and Maps   217

Endnotes   221

Index   231

About the Author   237

ACKNOWLEDGEMENTS

The many who have shared in this story include US Navy Armed Guard Seaman Ernest Bryan, my father, who provided personal handwritten journals, letters, and photographs that were written and taken during his 1943 World War II convoy voyages. His story includes accounts of his experiences told to his family, friends, and crewmates, some still living today.

And to the many other people, including friends and family who have supported me in this project, I owe a huge debt of gratitude. First and foremost, I would like to thank my husband Bill, an active volunteer member of the Commemorative Air Force, for his encouragement, assistance, editing support, and World War II military knowledge. And a special thanks to Mark Gegenheimer, a grandson of Ernest Bryan, who provided the artwork and graphic illustrations for this book. My thanks also go to Brennen Transier, great-grandson of Ernest Bryan, who kindly and patiently photographed the author.

German U-boat War Diaries, *Kriegstagebuch (KTB) U-565*, Secret German Command documents captured after the war by the British, were later shared by the United Kingdom Archives and stored with the US National Archives in College Park, Maryland. The documents provided *U-565* Korvettenkapitän Wilhelm Franken's account of his missions during that pivotal time in the North Atlantic. German war logs—regarded in Germany as legal documents—had to be signed personally by commanders every four hours. U-boat commanders also carried small observation books for recording personal information during patrols.

I want to thank Uwe Röttcher, who lives in Hannover-Langenhagen, Germany. He was a personal friend of crew members under the command of Wilhelm Franken aboard *U-565*. The private letters written by Wilhelm Franken during his U-boat patrols were graciously provided with Uwe's express written permission and with his desire to keep the story of Wilhelm Franken alive in the public memory.

Accounts of the oil tanker, SS *Esso Montpelier,* written by US Navy Armed Guard officers, were acquired from three 1943 Voyage Reports obtained from Naval Archives II, Naval Records Collection, Office of Naval Records and Library, College Park. These Voyage Reports provide detailed accounts of the convoy experiences for three convoys: UGS-4, UGS-7, and HX-242. These convoys traveled the North Atlantic from January 13 through July 15, 1943, during the Battle of the Atlantic. Accounts of German U-boat commanding officers and their sinking of Allied ships are derived from factual data obtained from multiple historical sources, including the US and UK National Archives, books, websites, and personal letters.

I thank US Navy Armed Guard veteran Francis B. Kent for his accounts of the Armed Guard life. Kent's stories were acquired from our conversations along with his journal, *The Way It Was*, with his express consent. I also thank Armed Guard veteran William Hollenback, a personal friend and crewmember with my father on the *Esso Montpelier* in 1943. William shared many personal stories, describing his convoy travels, hardships, and the heroic delivery of cargo during the Battle of the Atlantic.

John S. Westerlund, PhD, author of *Arizona's War Town: Flagstaff, Navajo Ordnance Depot, and World War II* and retired US Army artillery officer, provided invaluable support, as well as educating and mentoring me in the writing of this book. His guidance towards historical research at the National Archives in College Park and the study of critical military figures attached to the Atlantic Convoys of 1943 helped immensely in providing the backbone of this story.

Eric C. Rust, PhD, author of *U-Boat Commander Oskar Kusch: Anatomy of a Nazi-Era Betrayal and Judicial Murder* and West German Navy veteran, provided invaluable insight, advice, and editorial refinements surrounding the German U-boat service and its officers, as well as translations from German.

I also want to express my deepest gratitude to my personal friend and retired Navy Captain Alice Prucha for her accounts of Navy life and for providing editing support for naval terminology.

Additionally, my thanks go to two translators who greatly supported the German details of this story. The initial *German War Diary (Kriegstagebuch U-565)* German-to-English translations were graciously provided by Marilya Veteto Reese, PhD, a German professor at Northern Arizona University, Flagstaff, Arizona. I also wish to express appreciation to retired US Navy Captain Jerry Mason, founder and author of the website www.uboatarchive. net, for his precise and detailed military *U-565* log reports. Mason's translations from Wilhelm Franken's daily war diaries were freely given with additional knowledge and background, including U-boat photo contributions.

I also give special acknowledgment to the World War II history buffs who have made the Battle of the Atlantic and the U-boat force come alive in their user-friendly online archives, available for public access. The website www.uboat.net has been invaluable in providing the background of U-boats and their commanders. Information concerning Allied convoys, compiled by the late Lieutenant Commander Arnold Hague, RN, were placed online by Don Kindell on the website at www.convoyweb.org.uk. The stories of the Allied convoys and their sinkings, as told by crew members and ships masters' (captains') log reports, helped to capture the struggles and heroism of these war heroes.

And lastly, my sincere thanks go to the veteran crewmates of Ernest Bryan, past and current, who relived previous times and shared their insights and experiences. My personal interviews with these World War II veterans were most gratifying, and at times the stories shared would bring tears to my eyes while others left me with the utmost respect. The surviving heroes of those times are all quietly passing and becoming invisible to today's generations. Many of their own stories were never told. Their children and the generations to follow will never know the personal sacrifices of that war generation. My hope in sharing this story is to provide my family and their generations to follow with a better understanding of the lives of two warriors from opposing countries and cultures. It is my fervent hope that it will continue to be passed down and shared with future generations. The courage and sacrifice of these two men should serve as an inspiration for us all. Our World War II veterans and their memories are fading as the past generations leave only footprints behind.

May we never forget.

PREFACE

Some of us were fortunate to hear firsthand war stories told by our fathers and grandfathers. However, many men of previous generations never spoke of their war experiences and the lives they lived. They chose not to awaken the past and the painful memories associated with those times. Today we would call this PTSD.

My passion for researching and writing about past historical events and different cultures began with the stories my father told of his time spent in the military during World War II. As an armchair historian and genealogist, I've always been drawn to untold and personal stories from the past—stories we may not know or remember. The research and discovery of my father's World War II handwritten journals provided the catalyst to writing his story. The uncovering and understanding of the story of his younger years and his military background offered many of the insights contained in this book, as well as insights into the American patriotism he held for a lifetime. As a result of the subsequent discovery of a German U-boat commander's war diary and his personal letters, this story began with one man and ultimately evolved into two men's parallel stories on opposing sides of a global war.

This true story takes place during the World War II Battle of the Atlantic, specifically in the year 1943. This was the most prolonged battle of the war—the battle above and below the Atlantic Ocean and the Mediterranean Sea (1939-1945). The details of the story are based on an American seaman's journals and letters and the ship's log reports while he was deployed on merchant ship convoys and a German U-boat commander's war diary and battle logs during the same period. The battle accounts and details cover a specific six-month period when the action unfolded.

Included in the story are the words, phrases, slang, and military jargon used in 1943. Both the US and German Navy terminology and code words are written verbatim and are not always easy to follow. Readers may find some words archaic or outdated. To ensure authenticity, the actual verbiage and actions taken (as written by the men of this story) have not been altered. In cases of translation from German to English, certain words may have more than one meaning and were at the translator's discretion.

On April 19, 1943, US Navy Seaman Ernest Bryan and German U-boat Kapitänleutnant Wilhelm Franken crossed paths in the Mediterranean Sea. Reports and journals combine firsthand accounts of deadly combat from both men. Battle decisions made on board their vessels resulted in many lives being lost and many being saved. This isolated encounter gives a brief insight into the fears, courage, and heroism of two men and how their lives were forever changed.

This is their story.

Above and Below:
Silent Heroes of World War II

Prologue

Figure 1. This scene depicts Seaman Ernest Bryan witnessing the sinking of the *Sidi-Bel-Abbes* in the Mediterranean Sea after a U-boat torpedo attack. His wife experienced this moment in her dream while living in Miami at the same time the U-boat attack occurred.

In Miami, Florida, on April 20, 1943, at 2:50 a.m., a young woman, Vera Bryan, jolted awake in a panic from a disturbing dream about her husband. A loud explosion still echoed in her head. Her heart was pounding, and she could feel the heat of flames on her face. A haze of smoke was clouding her vision as she grappled with her fears. She realized then the possible death of her husband, on board a ship somewhere in the Atlantic. She wrote the date and time down for later reference.

Figure 2. Kapitänleutnant Wilhelm Franken, in command of *U-565* from March 1942 to October 1943. Franken was recognized for his bravery, leadership, and fighting spirit and for his U-boat successes.

Southern Spain and U-565

On April 19, 1943, while patrolling in the Mediterranean Sea off the southern coast of Spain, Kapitänleutnant Wilhelm Franken of *U-565* received a radio message at 2118 hours from the Befehlshaber der U-Boote (BdU Command Headquarters of the U-boat arm in Kiel, Germany). The message provided details of an enemy convoy that consisted of two transporters, thirty-two freighters, six tankers, and nine convoy escorts. They had crossed Ceuta, the north coast of Africa, earlier that day at approximately 1200 hours.

From previous convoy hunts, Franken was well aware of the convoy's direction and speculated he could correctly determine in advance the path the convoy would travel. The convoy would proceed from Ceuta on a

Mediterranean course. He concluded it could not go more southerly due to the proximity of the coast, and to save time it would not evade to the north. He decided to gamble and run ahead of the convoy to get to an improved attack position. KptLt. Wilhelm Franken and his *U-565* would be waiting for the convoy with a pre-dawn attack!

Figure 3. Ernest Bryan, a US Navy Armed Guard Signalman/Boatswain, completed three convoy crossings during the Battle of the Atlantic, January 13 through July 1, 1943. On board an oil tanker, his close encounter with *U-565* left him a lifetime patriot with unforgettable memories.

Early the next day, April 20, 1943, at 0750 hours, US Navy First Class (1/c) Signalman Ernest Bryan on board the oil tanker *Esso Montpelier* awoke with a start to a loud explosion. Alarms were blasting as he and the off-duty crew scrambled from their bunks and raced topside to their assigned battle stations.

When Ernest first reached the top deck of his ship, a second loud explosion hit. He searched the skies for enemy planes. Through the morning fog, Ernest could see billowing smoke and massive flames towering above his ship and against the horizon. It was then he saw a partial shape emerge—the vessel on the starboard beam of his tanker—blown in half. Wreckage and bodies covered the ocean. Ernest knew their convoy was under attack. Without the sounds of enemy planes, he knew the threat was not from above, but coming from the depths below. He raced to his battle station, adrenaline pumping, primed for attack.

CHAPTER ONE

America Enters World War II

"Everything turns upon the Battle of the Atlantic, which is proceeding with growing intensity on both sides. Our losses in ships and tonnage are very heavy and, vast as our shipping resources which we control, the losses cannot continue indefinitely without seriously affecting our war effort and our means of subsistence."

– Winston Churchill, April 9, 1941

On September 1, 1939, Germany invaded Poland. Two days later, both Britain and France, allies of Poland, declared war on Germany. World War II began in Europe on September 3, 1939. From that day forward, some of the most famous battles fought in western Europe and beyond followed and claimed millions of military and civilian lives on all sides.

The first casualty of war, less than eight hours later on September 3, was not German—but British. It was the passenger ocean liner the *Athenia,* carrying civilians from England to Canada. The *Athenia* was sunk by a German undersea boat (U-boat) in the Atlantic Ocean, just west of Ireland. *U-30* had assumed the ship was armed and belligerent and had attacked without warning. There were more than 1,200 passengers on board, and 118 lost their lives, including 29 Americans. This attack marked the beginning of the Battle of the Atlantic, as coined by Winston Churchill in February 1941. It has been called the "longest, largest, and most complex" naval battle in history, lasting the full duration of World War II. The six-year naval warfare pitted the German U-boats, aircraft, warships, and—later—Italian submarines against the Allied escort warships and convoys moving military equipment and supplies across the Atlantic. The war covered over four million square miles of ocean. Although Americans were killed in this first attack as a result of the *Athenia* tragedy, the United States remained neutral, not entering Europe's war.

At the beginning of World War II, the British Royal Navy was the most powerful in the world. It had the largest number of ships and a network of navy bases around the globe. Before mobilization, the strength of the British

Navy was 9,762 officers and 109,170 seamen. There were also 51,485 men in the Royal Fleet Reserve, 10,038 in the Royal Navy Reserve, 2,049 in the Royal Navy Auxiliary Reserves, and 6,180 in the Royal Naval Volunteer Reserve. Additionally, in September 1938, a year before declaring war, the British government, foreseeing a need to reinforce the Merchant Navy, had begun calling for civilian volunteers with experience at sea. Within the year, they had 13,000 volunteers, including navigation officers, engineers, deckhands, cooks, and stewards. Once war was declared, 12,000 officers and men of the existing Merchant Navy (many were members of the Royal Naval Reserve) applied to join the fighting services. Those numbers continued to climb. All those who served in the Merchant Navy were civilian volunteers who managed the logistical transportation of war cargo.

Seaman joining the Merchant Navy came from every part of the British Isles. By the end of the war, British merchant seamen rose in numbers to 22,490. More than 25,000 additional men, including men from China, the United States, Norway, Greece, the Netherlands, Denmark, Canada, Belgium, South Africa, Australia, and New Zealand, as well as thousands more from neutral countries, signed up. Throughout the war, ocean convoys crewed by Allied merchant seamen of many nations brought vital supplies to keep the war effort going. The most significant and crucial conflicts in which civilian merchant seamen were involved was the Battle of the Atlantic.

On April 9, 1940, seven months after the start of the war, Hitler's forces invaded Denmark and Norway. Code-named *Operation Weserübung* (Weser River exercise), the invasion was the opening operation of the Norwegian Campaign. Hitler then turned his attention to Belgium, the Netherlands, Luxembourg, and France, who possessed the most powerful army in Europe in 1940. Beginning on May 10, 1940, German forces, using the military tactic called *Blitzkrieg* (lightning war)—a brilliant tool, combining forceful and swift action with a concentration of offensive weapons (such as tanks, planes, and artillery)—quickly overran Belgium, the Netherlands, Luxembourg, and France within six weeks. The Netherlands was vital because it had essential ports used for shipping German supplies and supporting the war effort.

Also, on May 10, 1940, during Germany's invasion of western Europe, Winston Churchill became prime minister of Great Britain, succeeding Prime Minister Neville Chamberlain (1937-1940). By mid-June, three of the four countries had surrendered. France signed an armistice in late June 1940. Hitler then prepared to invade Great Britain.

Since Germany controlled much of the continent of Europe, Great Britain was unable to provide and obtain the materials it needed to wage war on its own. If Germany defeated the United Kingdom, the United States would be the last great democracy left in the world. Prime Minister Winston Churchill reached out for support to the United States and Canada. One of his most famous speeches delivered on June 4, 1940, to the House of Commons strengthened American sympathy for his cause. He stated,

> Even though large tracts of Europe and many old and famous States have fallen or may fall into the grip of the Gestapo and all the odious apparatus of Nazi rule, we shall not flag or fail. We shall go on to the end. We shall fight in France; we shall fight in the seas and oceans; we shall fight with growing confidence and growing strength in the air; we shall defend our island whatever the cost may be. We shall fight on the beaches; we shall fight on the landing grounds, we shall fight in the fields and in the streets, we shall fight in the hills; we shall never surrender.[1]

With the fight on land and ocean underway, Germany turned its attention to invading Great Britain by air. This next battle known as the Battle of Britain (July 10 to October 31, 1940) was the first major campaign in history that was fought entirely in the air. While the German Airforce, the Luftwaffe, was numerically superior, the Royal Air Force (RAF) had the advantage of land-based radar tracking. Additionally, they could better defend against attacks within familiar British territory. Despite German air superiority, Luftwaffe bombers incurred heavy losses to RAF Spitfire and Hurricane fighters. In September 1940, Hitler finally recognized the futility of the battle and postponed the invasion of Britain.

America, determined to stay out of Europe's war, remained neutral for more than two years. However, it was neutrality, not indifference. President Franklin Roosevelt saw Britain's survival as essential to American security and did everything possible to support Britain and their battle with Germany. He provided ammunition, fuel, aircraft, tanks, weapons, and food shipped via convoys. Unprotected convoys of merchant ships sailed from various points of the Western Hemisphere, carrying the critical items needed to support the war efforts across the Atlantic to Great Britain and the Soviet Union. Germany fought to control the sea lanes where American materials and cargo flowed across the Atlantic. The Allied purpose was not to engage and destroy the enemy in the Atlantic but to keep the delivery system going at whatever cost. Among America's contributions to the Allied cause, the production of cargo ships and warships topped the list. Even before the United States entered the war, they provided Britain with sixty cargo ships and fifty old World War I destroyers.

Although it was unofficial, in reality the United States was at war against Germany in the Atlantic Ocean in the latter part of 1941. On September 4, 1941, a German U-boat attacked the destroyer, USS *Greer* while on patrol in the North Atlantic. This was the first time a U-boat had fired at an American warship and the first time that an American warship returned fire. No damage occurred, but, as a result, President Roosevelt ordered the US Navy to shoot on sight, thereby officially sanctioning American attacks on German and Italian submarines in the Atlantic. Within two months, on October 31, 1941, a U-boat torpedoed and sank the first American destroyer USS *Reuben James* while it was escorting a convoy near Iceland, killing 115 American sailors.[2] Once again, although American lives were lost, President Roosevelt continued to remain neutral in Europe's war, declaring, "Let no man or woman thoughtlessly or falsely talk of America sending its armies to European fields."[3]

Figure 4. The first peacetime draft in US history began on September 16, 1940, more than a year before the United States entered World War II. It required all men between the ages of twenty-one and forty-five to register for the draft. Recruitment posters played an essential role in supporting the US military during the war. By late 1942, all men between eighteen and sixty-four years old were required to register. In December 1941, the US military enlisted 2.2 million soldiers. By the end of the war, thirty-six million men had registered for the draft.[4]

Thirty-eight days later, the United States declared war following the Japanese attack at Pearl Harbor, Hawaii. On December 8, 1941, the day after the devastating air raid, President Roosevelt went before the US Congress and asked for a formal declaration of war against Japan. President Roosevelt never asked for a declaration of war against Italy or Germany. Instead, four days after Japan's attack, Hitler and Italy—in support of their ally and bound by a promise to Japan—unhesitatingly declared war on the United States. Because a condition of war already existed between Germany and the United States in the Atlantic Ocean, Hitler had little to lose by making it official. President Roosevelt immediately declared, "In the future, US air and naval forces will protect all shipping in their waters of whatever flag close to the US safe zone."

World War II had thus reached truly global proportions with six major powers locked in combat across the continents and oceans of the world. Germany, Italy, and Japan—led by Hitler, Mussolini, and Tojo, respectively—were confronted by the countries of the Great Alliance under the leadership of the Big Three: Prime Minister Churchill, President Roosevelt, and Marshal Stalin.[5] The two warring sides were respectively referred to as the Axis and the Allies.

Before Pearl Harbor, German U-boats enjoyed success against the British Royal Navy and its Allies in the Atlantic. The "First Happy Time," as noted by U-boat crews, started in June 1940 and generally dated from the defeat of France in the North Atlantic and North Sea. According to various sources, it ended in October 1940, while others cited the end as April 1941 due to more reported sinkings of Allied ships.

German Navy Admiral Dönitz, a veteran of World War I, commanded the German U-boat force that posed a serious threat to Allied efforts in the Battle of the Atlantic. Although most Allied ships were equipped with sonar that could detect submerged U-boats, they were helpless when the Germans made nighttime surface attacks. Transatlantic convoys came under severe attack by U-boats employing the German tactic *Rudeltaktik,* created by Dönitz and referred to as "wolf packs," as a means to defeat the Allied convoy system. All nearby U-boats would encircle a convoy in groups of eight to twenty and attack as many vessels as possible to overwhelm the convoy escorts. It was a highly successful time for the Germans in 1940. U-boats sank 282 Allied ships totaling nearly 1.5 million tons in the North Atlantic and the North Sea. Even before the United States entered the war, the US merchant ships had already experienced the deadly impact of Europe's war. As early as November 1940, seventeen US merchant vessels were sunk, killing 200 civilian merchant seamen. [6]

Immediately following Hitler's declaration of war on the United States, American ships in the North Atlantic and elsewhere were determined to be fair game. On December 12, 1941, Admiral Dönitz unleashed his U-boat assault plan. This operation, appropriately named *Paukenschlag* (often translated as "drumbeat" or "drumroll," but it literally means "timpani beat"), commenced with an initial wave of surprise attacks on the US East Coast and Allied shipping.[7] The second "Happy Times" attacks coincided with Operation Drumbeat. Germany believed it could win the war by preventing the United States from supplying Britain with any additional war matériel and fuel.[8] Dönitz, the mastermind of the U-boat campaign, believed the US Navy was ill-prepared and ill-equipped to fight the well-trained U-boat fleet. He was correct! America's coastal defenses were unable to protect the eastern shoreline.

Only five long-range German U-boats were available for the first assault. Dönitz chose his best U-boat "aces" to command the first attacks. Each of the U-boats carried sealed orders to open after arriving in North American waters between Portland, Maine, and New York City, New York. The U-boats officially began their attacks on the highly vulnerable, solitary merchant ships traveling the weakly guarded sea-lanes near the American shore. The first attack occurred on January 12, 1942, when the British passenger steamer SS *Cyclops* was torpedoed and sunk about 300 miles east of Cape Cod by *U-123*.[9] More attacks followed, and the "Second Happy Time" or the "American shooting season," so named by U-boat crews, continued. The U-boats dominated the waters off the East Coast of North America until early August.

German U-boats patrolled the coast, safely submerged through the day and surfacing at night, attacking defenseless passenger ships and merchant vessels outlined against city lights in the background. Ships were sunk before they could head overseas with their cargo. The five U-boats, with a combined total of one hundred torpedoes and a couple of hundred men, completed a more than two-month campaign and achieved overwhelming success in sending American merchant ships and cargo to the bottom of the ocean. The initial operations off the East Coast sank twenty-five ships for a total of 156,939 tons. Also, the German submarine *U-123* sank an additional nine ships for a total of 53,173 tons, including a Norwegian and a British tanker. Hundreds of Allied lives were lost. According to German Navy reports, the U-boats' success was primarily due to the Allied ships' visible outlines against the coastal city lights, which made the ships sitting ducks.

Following the early success, Admiral Dönitz began sending shorter-range Type VII U-boats to the US East Coast for the second round of Operation Drumbeat. Next, a third wave of U-boats in *Operation Neuland* (New Land) reached its patrol area off the oil ports of the Caribbean and sank many oil tankers. Overall, the incredible seven-month German Navy operation, with its lightning-fast surprise attacks, sank over 609 vessels, totaling over 3.1 million tons. An estimated 5,000 seamen and passengers' lives were lost, more than twice the number of people who perished at Pearl Harbor.

The Japanese attack on Pearl Harbor and the declaration of war by Nazi Germany caught the US Navy unprepared for a two-ocean war. The Navy failed to organize the merchant ships into convoys in a timely fashion and was unable to provide adequate anti-submarine-warfare protection by either the US Navy or the US Army Air Corps. During this period, the US Navy and Coast Guard had only twenty ships—mostly cutters, patrol cutters, and gunboats—to defend the 1,500-mile US eastern seaboard. The Navy, however, was able to deploy 103 short-range operational aircraft to patrol the East Coast.

The United States struggled in response to the horrible loss of ships, cargo, and lives. The Navy's attention was still focused on Pearl Harbor.

The decision to implement convoys—groups of seagoing vessels traveling together for mutual support—came slowly, along with the Navy's protection and the prescribed blackout of coastal towns at night to make ships less visible. The failure of US pre-war planning was made even worse by the lack of any vessel suitable for convoy escort. According to the figures from the Maritime Commission and the Arming Merchant Ships Section in the Office of Naval Operations, the Unites States had only 1,340 cargo ships and tankers. Additionally, escort vessels traveled at relatively slow speeds, carried a large number of depth-charges, had to be highly maneuverable, and were required to stay on station for long periods. Fleet destroyers, however, were equipped for high speed and offensive action but were not an ideal design for anti-submarine warfare.

Figure 5. The Office of War Information's drive to limit talk about the war in both the public and private arenas of American life was central to maintaining national security. Silence meant security. The campaign ads encouraged Americans to be discreet in their communication and thus to prevent information from being leaked to the enemy.

By February 1942, the extent of the loss of ships, lives, and cargo had become known to the public. The "Loose Lips Sink Ships"[10] propaganda campaign began at this time. However, it was not designed to prevent German agents' knowledge of American vessels' sailing times, rather to keep American civilian morale up by reducing communication about how many ships were sunk during Operation Drumbeat.

That month, despite US efforts to censor information about the sinkings, six merchant ships in New York harbor refused to sail until they had adequate protection. And the Navy—unprepared, unorganized, and untrained in submarine warfare—remained dangerously slow to respond to the U-boat threat.[11] The losses continued, taking their toll on lives and cargo for almost "6 months of secret terror in the Atlantic."[12] In 1942, Allied losses from the Dönitz submarine campaign rose to 900 vessels, totaling 6,250,000 gross tons.[13]

Winston Churchill understood the gravity of the situation and knew that Admiral Dönitz had found fertile ground. Though hard-pressed from fighting on several fronts, the British sent some corvettes (small warships) to help the American cause. The situation was critical. The problem of moving vast numbers of men and supplies across submarine-infested waters, compounded by enemy aircraft, became a high-priority focus for the United States.

While much of the year 1942 proved disastrous for the unprotected merchant ships and seamen, this had not always been the case. During World War I, 384 US merchant vessels also carried guns and armed Navy personnel under the limited authority of a US Navy Armed Guard branch in charge of protecting the ships and personnel aboard. The program was successful. However, this branch was disbanded in 1919. In 1942, Allied merchant ships were in desperate need of a reestablished US Navy Armed Guard but larger and more powerful than that of World War I.

In fact, the Navy had started to reestablish the Armed Guard, training a few people in gunnery in the spring of 1941. Still, the program made little progress in developing the vast administrative organization necessary to handle the US Navy Armed Guard Service under war conditions. Improvements slowly began on January 31, 1942, once program authority was redirected to the Arming Merchant Ships Section in the Fleet Maintenance Division of the Office of the Chief of Naval Operations. Operational standards for merchant ships and safety measures were enforced. Deck strengthening and gun foundations were installed for purposes of arming merchant ships and troop transports. The standard set of weapons for an armed merchant ship going into combat zones was established: a 5-inch/38-caliber dual-purpose stern (deck) gun; a 3-inch/50-caliber anti-aircraft gun; and eight 20mm MK II (a Mark version) machine guns. Some merchant ships were also retrofitted with 5-inch/50-caliber anti-aircraft guns. The anti-aircraft weapons were designed for air defense and were effective against close-range U-boat surface attacks but were ineffective against submerged U-boats.[14]

Figure 6. Aerial view of a "Convoy at Sea." Groups of ships formed together as a convoy for mutual protection and safety while crossing the Atlantic Ocean to Casablanca, Morocco, with valuable cargo, supplies, weapons, oil, and troops needed for the global war efforts.

The standard complement of US Navy personnel assigned for the protection of merchant vessels was: one officer, twenty-four gunners, and three communications specialists for a total of twenty-eight Armed Guards. The Navy made every effort to give each ship the best possible protection. Additionally, the organization and formation of large convoys were supported with an increased number of escort warships for safety during travel.

In April 1942, the desperate situation of the merchant ships began to improve. The US Navy implemented a limited convoy system in which ships traveled along the East Coast only during daylight hours. At night, merchant ships put into sheltered harbors with city blackout orders, resulting in an immediate reduction of Allied shipping losses off the East Coast. The convoy system later extended to the Gulf of Mexico with similar dramatic effects. Dönitz withdrew his U-boats to seek easier pickings elsewhere.[15]

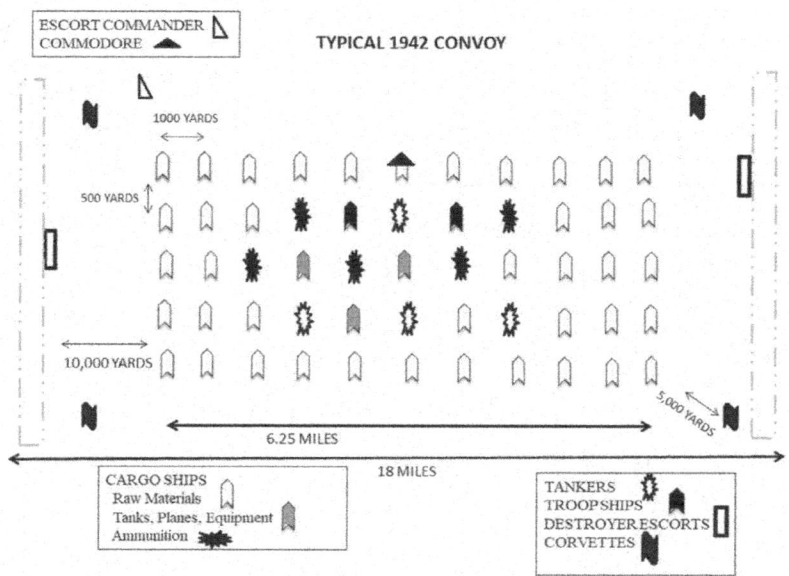

Figure 7. In typical formation, the convoy was escorted by two destroyers and four corvettes. Two corvettes patrolled the rear, and two patrolled the flank. The two destroyers patrolled the front in elliptical patterns to prevent attacks. The convoy's vessels were deployed only five-deep, thereby minimizing the number exposed to flank attacks. Oil tankers, troop transports, ammunition ships, and vessels loaded with tanks, guns, planes, and other vital cargo traveled inside the formation. Ammunition ships were never positioned next to one another or next to oil tankers for fear a torpedo hit might set off a chain reaction of explosions or fires.

Full convoys were in operation by mid-May 1942. There were usually two types of convoys: "fast" ones that proceeded at 9 knots (10.6 mph) and "slow" ones that traveled at 7.5 knots (8.63 mph). Each convoy was restricted to moving at the speed of the slowest vessel within the convoy. Typical Allied convoy formations were organized in a rectangular pattern with escort ships stationed around the perimeter. Ammunition ships, oil tankers, and troop transports positioned themselves inside the protection of the escort ships' perimeter for relative safety. The spacing of ships was best maintained at 1,000 yards apart and 500 yards between bow and stern. In calm weather, ships within a convoy had little difficulty keeping in orderly rows and columns. However, when U-boats attacked, the precise spacing was almost impossible to maintain.

Military destroyer escorts were called upon to protect the convoys. Convoys typically spread over six miles with destroyer protection spaced over eighteen miles. These escorts specifically became the armed vessel guards for more than just assuring the safety of the supply ships. They were also used to search for, hunt down, and sink German U-boats. The convoy's Merchant Marine commodore, who was responsible for the merchant vessels and communications, maintained his position front and center. The escort ship's US Navy captain also rode up front on the convoy's portside. Under U-boat attacks, the escort captain took charge of the entire convoy, issuing orders to the commodore.[16] Fortunately, the convoy system turned out to be the most effective defense against U-boats.

America's entry into the war had significant consequences for the U-boat campaign. Slowly the Americans continued to gain knowledge and sharpened their skills in anti-submarine warfare. Finally, a year and a half after the United States entered the war, the shipyards were building ships faster than the enemy was able to sink them. The United States began building up the most impressive fleet of naval vessels the world had ever known.

CHAPTER TWO

Ten Years Earlier in Florida

"Drag your thoughts away from your troubles… by the ears, by the heels, or any other way you can manage it."

-Mark Twain

I n 1932, ten years before his World War II military enlistment, Ernest Bryan, a young boy living in Miami, Florida, was gaining his own first-hand experiences in loss of life, hard times, and feelings of abandonment.

Figure 8. Ernest Bryan, shown in 1934 at the age of 14, was the youngest child in the family with five other siblings.

Ernest Bryan's father, Enoch, was born in 1873 and was raised on a farm in Richlands, North Carolina. In later years, he moved to Brunswick, Georgia, and married Tempa Hires in 1897. In Georgia, Enoch, a ship's carpenter and cabinet maker, raised nine children with Tempa. The loss of three children from sickness and accidents made for very tough times.

Shortly after World War I ended in 1918, Enoch and his family relocated to Miami, Florida, where Enoch continued to work in the lumber industry. His youngest son, Ernest, was born September 19, 1920. (Early birth records show the year 1921.)

When Ernest was eleven years old, his mother became very ill and was not expected to live. The youngest of the six surviving children, Ernest sat in the living room waiting at his mother's closed bedroom door with his four older brothers—Leon, Phil, Paul, and Enoch. When the door finally opened, their father stepped out of the bedroom and closed the door. Enoch Bryan Sr. gruffly informed his sons, "Your mother is no longer with us," and left the house. Ernest's older sister, Edna Mae, escorted her brothers into the bedroom to say their final farewells to their mother. Tempa Angeline Bryan died on September 13, 1932, at the age of fifty-three from tuberculosis.

From that point on, Ernest's life would considerably change. His father Enoch told him that, while on her death bed, his mother had pleaded with him to put Ernest up for adoption after she died. She believed Ernest, at the age of eleven, needed to have a mother. She felt the other boys, several years older than Ernest, would be fine. During this period (1929-1941), the Great Depression was a difficult time in America, both economically and socially. Unemployment was at 25 percent. Millions of people suffered from extreme poverty, often unable to feed themselves or their families.

Ernest's sister, Edna Mae, was thirty-four years old and married with a child of her own. His oldest brother Leon, who was now twenty-eight years old, was also married and also had a child. Neither was in a position to raise their youngest brother. Ernest's brother Enoch Jr. was fourteen years old and moved in with his sister while his other brothers, Phil and Paul, continued to live with their father, working in construction and carpentry. Enoch chose not to put Ernest up for adoption. Instead, he decided the best course of action was to send his youngest son to his father's farm in North Carolina where Enoch's half sister and her family lived. Ernest's aunt agreed to raise

Ernest with her children. Enoch packed up Ernest and his meager belongings and put him on a train headed for Onslow County, North Carolina. For the next several years, Ernest lived with his aunt, uncle, and cousins. He completed his eighth-grade schooling while working on the farm where tobacco was the Bryan family's primary "cash crop." Ernest felt fortunate that his father refused to put him up for adoption and looked forward to the day he could return home to Florida.

The death of his mother, the abrupt separation from his father and brothers shortly after his mother's death, and the removal from his childhood homelife created a deep void for the eleven-year-old. His young world underwent vast changes, as he adapted to the hard work and tough lessons that come with family farming. North Carolina's farmers were producing plenty of cash crops like cotton and tobacco, but, during the Great Depression, they were not making enough money from these crops to afford food.

As with most everyone, there are memories of traumatic events that will never be forgotten. Ernest was no different and spoke of one such memory. He and one of his cousins were assigned specific work responsibilities, as was everyone working on the farm. Their job was to feed logs into the fire next to the flue in the tobacco-curing barn. "My main responsibility was keeping the fires hot," he said. They were given strict instructions to "never let the fires go out." The loss of any crops would hurt the family business. One early morning, Ernest and his cousin were both found sound asleep in the tobacco drying barn with the fire almost out. The thrashing both boys received left an impression on Ernest. "You can bet I never slept a wink again when I was tending the fires." This lesson would serve him well in his future military life.

After three years, Ernest left his life on the farm and returned to his father's home in Miami. His father had remarried and expected Ernest to earn his keep while living at his home. Ernest's older brothers and sister were married and living their own lives. He learned at an early age how to survive on his own. Hard work continued for the teenage boy, and high school was not an option. Instead, he worked many jobs, including shoveling coal on a steam train, hauling blocks of ice to houses, and working in the dockyards. Ships and ocean sailing had always been an interest and desire for Ernest. According to stories told by his cousins, he lied about his age when he signed on to work on a merchant freighter in 1936 at the age of fifteen years. He told tales of working as a deckhand for six months aboard a merchant ship bound for China.

Figure 9. Ernest Bryan's childhood home at 1393 N.W. 31st Street, Miami, Florida. His father, a carpenter, and older brothers helped to build the house in the 1920s. Today, the house no longer exists, and the lot is now vacant.

Ernest's life took a new direction at age seventeen when he met the love of his life at the local Miami beach where he and several friends were visiting. Vera McDaniel, one of the most beautiful girls he had ever seen, with her long, black, wavy hair and green eyes, was a Miami Edison High School girl. He knew she was going to be the only woman for him. Vera saw a good looking, charismatic, adventurous young man. Vera, an only child, lived with her mother and grandmother in Miami.

Within a year, Ernest left the merchant ship and life of travel and married Vera on January 14, 1938. They moved into a small Miami apartment and welcomed a baby girl on October 4, 1938. Ernest worked on local construction jobs with his father and older brothers doing carpentry. He hoped to be a carpenter like his father someday. When construction work became scarce, Ernest started working as a mechanic for a relative at N.D. Nelson Service Station in Miami. A quick learner, he excelled as a mechanic and worked long hours to support his new family. However, Ernest and Vera's marriage started to unravel as their financial situation worsened. They could no longer afford their apartment. They moved in with Vera's mother in Miami to limit expenses.

Ernest and Vera were suffering like many others during the late 1930s as the Great Depression became America's most severe economic downturn. In 1941, the onset of World War II would change America's economy for the better and end the depression.

CHAPTER THREE

Ready to Serve His Country

"December 7th, 1941 — a date which will live in infamy"

-Franklin D. Roosevelt

In December 1941, after the Japanese attack on Pearl Harbor, men from all over the United States began enlisting in the military. The shock and anger resulting from the attack on American soil trumpeted the call to arms to men from all walks of life and backgrounds. Within a week, the German declaration of war against the United States presented another horrific turn of events. The US Navy began to expand rapidly, enlisting young men anxious for revenge. They wanted to do their part. Ernest and two of his brothers, Paul and Enoch Jr., were prepared to leave their families to join the military.

The need for a militarized naval construction force to build advance bases in war zones became evident after the attack on Pearl Harbor. On December 28, 1941, naval construction battalions were created, and on January 5, 1942, the recruitment of skilled construction workers began. Ernest's brother Paul enlisted in the Seabees Construction Battalion, working for the US Navy as a construction worker, replacing private construction companies. He was sent to a training center where he completed basic training and a general introduction to the Navy. Paul, a skilled carpenter, was deployed overseas and tasked to build military bases. Ernest's other brother Enoch enlisted in the US Army Corps of Engineers on April 16, 1942, working in a task force on the secret development of the atomic bomb.

On January 26, 1942, at the age of twenty-one, Ernest Bryan joined the Navy in Jacksonville, Florida, where he began basic training. Here he was taught Navy tradition, discipline, and close-order drills; was tested for intelligence and aptitude; and most importantly, was inoculated against diseases he might have exposure to wherever he was likely to be sent abroad.

This introductory period lasted for sixteen weeks. Ernest went through additional specialized training as a signalman, learning specific duties in visual communication. He studied Morse code, semaphore flag signaling, and alphabetic and numeric signal-flag recognition.

Once completing basic training, men were assigned to Navy shore duty or warships. Others were assigned to the US Navy Armed Guard that served aboard Allied merchant ships, protecting the ship as well as the crew of volunteer civilians. At the beginning of 1942, there was no ocean or sea anywhere on the planet where merchant shipping was free from hazards. Based on Ernest's past merchant ship deckhand experience, he either volunteered or was assigned to the US Navy Armed Guard. Enlistees dreaded the assignment as Armed Guard because of the constant dangers associated with the non-military vessels. Merchant ships were slow and unwieldy and were priority targets for enemy submarines and planes. Furthermore, merchant ships were among the last to receive updated equipment.

Figure 10. Seaman First Class (S1/c) Signalman
Ernest Bryan, US Navy Armed Guard, 1942.

One of Ernest's future shipmates, Seaman First Class (S1/c) William Hollenback, decided to volunteer for the Armed Guard while he was attending Navy boot camp in Bainbridge, Maryland. There, the US Navy Training Center was located on the bluffs of the northeast bank of the Susquehanna River. Years later, he recalled, "I was only seventeen and, after eight weeks, was ready for anything to get out of boot camp hell." He added, laughing, "I did not have a clue what I was getting myself into."[17]

Figure 11. Ernest Bryan (left) during Armed Guard gunnery training in Gulfport, Mississippi, in 1942, with a friend nicknamed "Blue" whom he met during training. Both men are holding standard Navy-issue M-1 Garand semi-automatic rifles with bayonets.

Men assigned to the Armed Guard traveled for additional training to one of three schools: Little Creek, Virginia; San Diego, California; or Gulfport, Mississippi. Ernest attended the Gulfport school for gunnery and weapons training. The primary goal was to teach men to shoot accurately and rapidly with a 5-inch/38-caliber gun, a 3-inch/50-caliber AA gun, and 20mm machine guns, practicing on air and surface targets. Each of the primary schools also had an anti-aircraft training center nearby and would send men out on ships for anti-aircraft and surface-firing practice. Men from the schools could thus supplement their training by the actual firing of anti-aircraft guns before they completed the Armed Guard course. Upon completion, they then moved on to one of the Armed Guard centers for assignment. The combat readiness and success of the officers and men of the World War II US Navy Armed Guard can be attributed to this extensive training.

"There were three Navy Armed Guard assignment centers: Brooklyn, New York; New Orleans, Louisiana; and Treasure Island, California," stated Francis Kent, World War II US Navy Armed Guard veteran. Although the Armed Guard was primarily men who handled the guns on merchant ships, not everyone dealt with weapons. There were signalmen, radiomen, a coxswain, and even a few pharmacist mates. "I was assigned as a radioman," Kent said. Also, virtually every Armed Guard crew was commanded by a commissioned officer—in most cases, a young ensign or lieutenant junior grade recently removed from a college campus. The Armed Guard officer had the status of a commanding officer in the US Navy. Regardless of rank or rating, these men shared the same hardships. "Today, they share their memories," explained Kent.

"One requisite of Armed Guards was that they be in good physical condition. They must have good eyes, ears, and teeth. They must be able to swim. However, above all, they must be people who had their hearts in their work, who loved their country and were willing to sacrifice even their lives for it if necessary. The Armed Guard was no place for the never-do-well, the malcontent, or the loafer," according to Kent.[18] The training was tough and demanding. Good health was a necessity since there were no medical doctors on board the merchant ships.

Ernest Bryan was well qualified for this branch of the Navy and was assigned to duty in the Brooklyn Armed Guard Center. This center was used explicitly for ship assignments sailing in the Atlantic Ocean and the Mediterranean Sea. The other two centers, New Orleans and Treasure Island, were for assignments in the Gulf of Mexico and the Pacific Ocean, respectively. These centers were the wartime duty stations of Armed Guard personnel when they were not at sea. Once Ernest was assigned to active duty, he felt prepared to defend his country even if it included sacrificing his life. However, most recruits, including Ernest, were not aware that the Armed Guard was considered the most dangerous job in the Navy, especially in specific geographic areas in the early years of the war. The casualty rate grimly rivaled the casualty rate of any of the Armed Forces during World War II.[19]

As Kent expressed, "If it were not for the Navy Armed Guard crews and other Armed Guard personnel, many more ships, cargo, and merchant seamen would have been lost and very likely so would the war." The Armed Guard's two mottos, "We Aim to Deliver" and "Don't Give Up the Ship," were behind their courageous efforts to deliver the cargo needed to support the war.[20]

After completing training with the Navy, Ernest received his orders to report for combat on his first Allied merchant ship convoy. He was assigned as a seaman first class (S1/c) signalman. Ernest Bryan would finally put his completed basic training and Armed Guard skills into wartime service. The convoy's departure date corresponded to the halfway mark of the Battle of the Atlantic. The battle at sea would have devastating consequences for both the Axis and Allied forces.

Meanwhile, in early November 1942, American forces made a surprise landing on the coast of French North Africa supported by British warships and aircraft and US merchant ships.

The ships defended by Armed Guards brought the troops, munitions, air support, and supplies necessary to effect the landing. These merchant ships were the spearhead of a much larger movement of merchant ships needed to build up the logistical support and matériel for the Allies' big push into Sicily and Italy. The Armed Guard played an essential and praiseworthy role in the North African operation.[21]

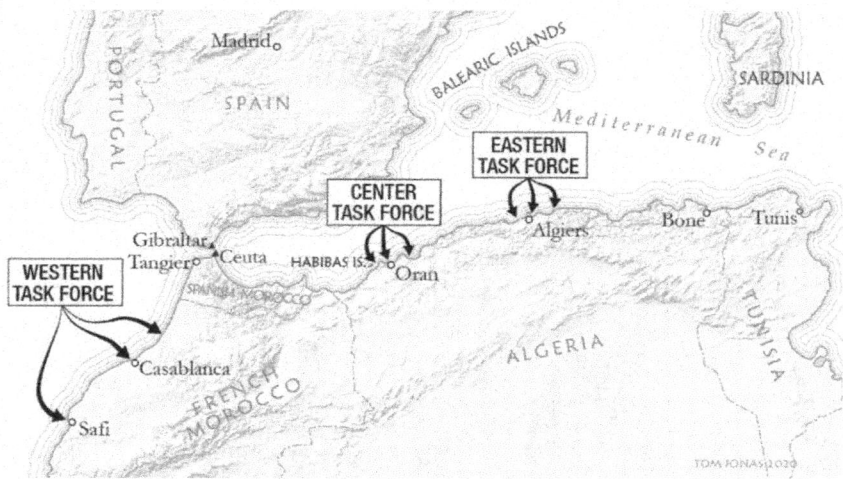

Figure 12. On November 8, 1942, the Allies launched Operation Torch, a three-pronged attack on Casablanca (Western), Oran (Center), and Algiers (Eastern). To gain a foothold in West Africa, they would push east to assist Montgomery's campaign against Rommel.

The attack was the first joint United States-British operation of World War II and was placed under the overall command of Lieutenant General Dwight Eisenhower.[22] Casablanca, the principal French Atlantic naval base, was captured from the Germans after a short siege. Oran surrendered along with Algiers. The three-pronged assault, named Operation Torch, established Allied footholds at Oran, Algiers, and Casablanca. The rapid move toward Tunis, complemented by Montgomery's assault from the east, ultimately resulted in an Allied victory. Operation Torch was the first US assault in the European Theatre and included the first American airborne operation of the war.

This Axis defeat resulted in a change in command of the German Navy. In January 1943, two months following the surprise Anglo-American landing in North Africa, Hitler promoted Dönitz to commander in chief of the German Navy. His promotion underlined the importance Hitler attached to the developing U-boat offensive in northwestern waters. Newly promoted Grand Admiral Dönitz immediately directed his efforts towards increased U-boat production, as well as improved design. German scientists also worked on methods to boost U-boat defenses. The number of U-boats in the Atlantic rose steadily. Wolf-pack attacks against Mediterranean and North Atlantic convoys were successful. Conditions in the primary naval warfare zone, the North Atlantic, were again very favorable for the Germans. However, Dönitz recognized that the enemy air force was, at that time, the most significant problem for the U-boat command.[23]

The threat posed by German U-boats to the Atlantic lifeline was critical and gave eminent importance to winning what Churchill had christened the "Battle of the Atlantic." U-boats were such a threat that Churchill commented that it was the only time in World War II that he thought Britain would have to contemplate surrendering.[24]

Ernest's first convoy duty followed in the wake of Operation Torch. The Armed Guard had only one—but an extremely difficult one—mission: to defend merchant ships and transports from enemy air, surface, and submarine attacks. It was quite evident that the most destructive element against merchant ships at this time was the U-boat. About eight times as many ships were sunk by German U-boats as were destroyed by planes. Although able to drive off a bomber, merchant ships were not armed to destroy submarines. However, every merchant ship was armed with a gun and was capable of sinking a U-boat if the enemy chose to engage in a close surface combat.[25] And if a torpedo was sighted in time, accurate shooting might destroy it before it hit the ship. Ultimately, it was the responsibility of the escort vessels and any Allied-friendly aircraft to deal death blows to U-boats. The Armed Guards' primary duties, therefore, were standing watch, operating guns, and maintaining weapons and defensive equipment. They had nothing to do with operating the merchant ships. Those responsibilities belonged to the merchant seamen, although the Armed Guards greatly assisted in fighting fires and salvage operations. Armed Guards were expected to live up to the highest standards and traditions of the Navy. The Armed Guards could only abandon ship when its sinking was imminent or when manning their weapons was impossible.[26]

Crossing the North Atlantic in winter conditions was another significant event in Ernest's life. His first merchant ship experience presented a bewildering situation, not at all like what he had expected when he joined the Navy. Men of the Armed Guard served on cargo ships, tankers, troopships, and other types of merchant vessels. Merchant ships lacked the creature comforts that were an integral part of warships: the services of a doctor, paymaster, ship's store, recreational facilities, mail clerks, and a sense of pride in belonging on a US Navy vessel with its rigid routine. Some of the newly assigned Armed Guard men had never spent any time at sea but suddenly found themselves responsible for the security and protection of experienced merchant seamen.

Aboard ship, the merchant and Navy crews had separate sleeping and eating quarters. Part of the Navy crew had their quarters amidships, divided between port and starboard; the remaining quarters were located at the ship's stern. For those in the aft quarters, there was the constant vibration of the ship's engine and propeller shaft with which to contend. In heavy seas, the stern would come out of the water and vibrate violently as the exposed propeller chopped incessantly at the thin air.[27]

In some cases, merchant ship crewmen displayed hostile attitudes and resentment toward the Armed Guard crew due to the latter's lack of experience. The command structure aboard the merchant ships could also be a problem area. There were two sets of command: merchant and Navy. Inexperienced Armed Guard officers freshly out of college were placed in charge of shipboard security and took command from the merchant ship master (captain) in combat situations. The Navy officer in charge had a tremendous responsibility while at sea, given there was no other senior military officer on board to consult. Unlike ships of the fleet, there were no medical personnel assigned to the men on board. Occasionally a pharmacist's mate might be aboard, but most medical problems were handled by the Armed Guard officer with whatever remedies he could find in his medicine chest. Should a severe medical problem arise, a doctor from an escort ship might be sent over. If that was not an option, the patient had to wait until his ship reached port. For the Navy officer in charge, the health, efficiency, and safety of the men on board the merchant ship depended on how well the ship's two crews worked together.

Up to this point, Bryan's training had prepared him for what to expect when engaging the enemy. But never seeing the enemy left him with many concerns about the unknown. Crews never knew when the call to battle stations might suddenly shatter an "uneventful" watch. With the dangers on the sea, below the sea, and in the air, courage was hard-earned. Anxiety and fear were in the background—always present, sometimes more to the fore, sometimes less—but never really displaced. Ernest was soon to come face-to-face with the fears and anxiety that came with convoy travels during the Battle of the Atlantic. Also, his new struggling marriage was close to an end, and he felt this departure would be the final blow. The separation from his young wife and daughter would cause lifelong abandonment issues for both himself and his loved ones.

CHAPTER FOUR

Convoy UGS-4: SS *Esso Montpelier*

They that go down to the sea in ships that do business in great waters;

These see the works of the Lord, and his wonders in the deep.

For he commandeth and raiseth the stormy wind which lifted up the waves thereof.

They mount up to the heaven, they go down again to the depths...

-PSALM 107:23-26

T he War Shipping Administration (WSA) was an emergency US government agency established two months after the attack on Pearl Harbor. The WSA had enormous shipping responsibilities that included the purchase or requisition of vessels for wartime use. When vessels of the Esso (Standard Oil name shortened to SO, then written as Esso, and today known as Exxon) fleet were chartered to the WSA, the SS *Esso Montpelier*'s trade route had been in the Gulf of Mexico and East Coast waters from July 1940 to November 1942. Upon completion of the vessel's 1942 scheduled deliveries, the oil tanker once again arrived on the East Coast of the United States for its new 1943 wartime assignment to North Africa.

On January 13, 1943, just two months after the Allies landed in North Africa, Ernest Bryan began duty on his first of three convoys from New York's Army Corps Port of Embarkation (NYPOE) as an Armed Guard aboard the *Esso Montpelier* traveling to the Mediterranean Sea. The "UG" (United States - Gibraltar) convoys were a series of eastbound transatlantic convoys from the United States carrying food, ammunition, and military hardware to the US Army in North Africa and subsequently in southern Europe. These convoys assembled in Hampton Roads, Virginia, near the mouth of Chesapeake Bay and terminated in various North African locations as Axis forces retreated. The *Esso Montpelier,* part of convoy UGS-4 (United States-Gibraltar Slow), left New York assigned to a destination of Oran, Algeria, with 70,148 barrels of fuel oil consigned to the British Admiralty. The destination on cargo documents was shown as "At sea." Convoy records list the names of forty-seven merchant ships (including two oil tankers) and six escorts assigned to various destinations, including Casablanca, Oran, Gibraltar, and Malta. (Appendix I (a) provides the information about each ship traveling in Convoy UGS-4.)

SS *Esso Montpelier*, 1940-1952

Figure 13. The SS (steamship) *Esso Montpelier*, a US oil tanker built in 1940 by the Federal Shipbuilding and Dry Dock Company at Kearny, New Jersey, was a single-screw vessel of 13,100 tons and 450 feet in length and 66 feet in breadth. Owned by Standard Oil of New Jersey, the oil tanker had a cargo capacity of 105,415 barrels. Her turbine engine, supplied with steam by two water-tube boilers, developed 3,300 shaft horsepower and gave the *Esso Montpelier* a speed of 12.7 knots. Her sister ships were the *Esso Bayonne, Esso Bayway, Esso Boston, Esso Houston,* and *Esso Concord.*

One of many merchant oil tankers, the *Esso Montpelier* delivered vital fuel cargo on convoys to the North African invasion forces. Of all the products Britain needed for survival, oil was crucial and had to come from overseas. This placed oil tanker fleets in the extremely vital category, as well as making them the most desirable targets for U-boats. Winston Churchill's instructions were to draw as much oil as possible from America, thus avoiding the long haul from the Persian Gulf around the capes of South Africa. Besides fuel, the *Esso Montpelier* also carried other critical cargo as needed for the war effort. In addition, the oil tanker transported American two-engine fighter planes known as the P-38 Lightning, used by the US Army and other Allied air forces, along with large cargo boxes of aircraft accessories and spare gas tanks. The P-38s were mostly used in the Pacific Theater through the middle of 1942. Later, the majority of P-38 squadrons were sent to Britain and some to North Africa where they aided the Allies in gaining air superiority over the Mediterranean. The P-38 was used for its speed and long-range and had extensive service as a bomber escort. Despite the dangerous routes across the turbulent sea, the oil tanker *Esso Montpelier* once again made its way from New York to the Mediterranean Sea and into Casablanca, Gibraltar, and Algiers in the wake of Operation Torch.

Following the landings of Operation Torch, Churchill, Roosevelt, and their military staffs met from January 13 to 24, 1943, in Casablanca, Morocco, to discuss strategy and follow-on plans. Although invited, Stalin was unable to leave Russia to attend on account of the huge Battle of Stalingrad, which he was directing. This conference was the first prolonged discussion between the two allies in which a complete agreement was reached between the leaders and staff. War plans for 1943 against Germany, Italy, and Japan were reviewed theater by theater, taking advantage of the favorable turn of events at the close of 1942.

During the meeting, the Allies decided to make the defeat of the U-boats a top priority objective. "U-boat warfare takes the first place in our thoughts," stressed Churchill. At the end of the ten-day Casablanca Conference (code-named SYMBOL), a general strategic program for 1943 was laid out. The most notable achievement of the conference was the decision to demand unconditional surrender from Germany and Japan. Unconditional surrender excluded the possibility of a negotiated peace. The Battle of the Atlantic, one of the lengthiest campaigns lasting the full duration of World War II, was also among the costliest. The stakes could not have been higher. Plans were immediately put into action.

Many of the warships used during Operation Torch were no longer needed in the Mediterranean. They were then placed on convoy escort duty in the Atlantic. The new additions significantly improved the convoys' ability to reach their destinations safely. Additionally, Liberty ships (simple, low-cost cargo ships) built in US shipyards could be constructed in just a few months. Soon the United States was producing more vessels than the U-boats could sink. From 1942 through 1945, US shipyards built 5,592 merchant ships, of which 2,710 were Liberty ships, 414 were the faster "Victory" ships, 651 were tankers, 417 were standard cargo ships (an emergency-built class of cargo ship), and the remaining 1,400 were military or specialty type ships.[28] By March 1943, additional anti-submarine resources and newly formed US escort carrier groups were stationed in the mid-Atlantic.

At this time, most escort warships such as destroyers were armed with new "hedgehog" anti-submarine weapons to supplement the depth charge. The hedgehogs, developed by the Royal Navy, could launch up to twenty-four small depth charges over a wide area and proved to be devastating weapons against detected U-boats. Allied scientists focused their efforts and furthered the development of anti-submarine weapons and detection equipment for improved defense of the convoys.[29]

Additionally, Roosevelt provided sixty-one long-range bombers (B-24 Liberators) to the RAF. This gave the convoys much greater aerial cover. The aircraft were fitted with Air to Surface Vessel (ASV) radar. This allowed a plane to spot a U-boat on the surface, but the U-boat could not detect ASV on its radar receiver. Therefore, a plane could attack a surfaced U-boat with the knowledge that the submarine did not know it was about to be attacked. Increased Allied air patrols successfully sank U-boats resulting in forty submarines being destroyed in the first quarter of 1943 alone. The anti-submarine Liberator bombers with their extended range played an instrumental role in closing the mid-Atlantic gap (an area halfway between England and Canada that could not be reached by land-based aircraft) in the Battle of the Atlantic. By mid-1943, convoys were having far greater success in reaching their destination in Britain.

Ernest's first convoy from January 13 through March 12, 1943, was part of a critical but dangerous mission when German U-boats were on the prowl. He would be at sea on board the oil tanker *Esso Montpelier* when the U-boats were still the most dangerous and were claiming significant losses of Allied merchant ships and the lives of military and civilian seamen. Ship crew members grimly relayed visual reports of torpedoed oil tankers as "…

the heat from a burning tanker could be felt at a range of 1,500 yards, and the fire could go on burning for hours." At other times, a stricken tanker might "erupt like a volcano and be gone in an instant." Ernest, like many other fellow seamen, would be putting his life in harm's way.

The *Esso Montpelier* would provide Ernest with many new experiences and challenges. Many of the lessons were not so pleasant, especially while "learning the ropes." As a signalman, his duty was to be on the bridge during all weather conditions, from sunrise until after sunset. Other lessons included humorous memories of life on board ship with the civilian merchant marine Allies and the Armed Guard crew working together.

Ernest recalled one of his first morning muster calls and, with a sheepish grin, relived an embarrassing situation. While standing at attention topside on the tanker with the other crew members, the officer in charge yelled, "Bryan!" Ernest promptly responded, "Yes, Sir?" The officer then commanded, "Hawse your anchor!" The officer repeated the command, "Bryan, hawse your anchor!" With a perplexed look and unclear of the order, Ernest hesitantly responded, "Sir, it's fine, sir!" There were muffled laughs from the other seamen at this point. Ernest belatedly understood the requirement of the command. The command "hawse" required the arrangement of the ship's anchor cables (or hawsers) used in mooring or towing a vessel. He immediately arranged the hawsers. For Ernest, it was an embarrassing mistake for a newly assigned Navy seaman, never to be repeated or forgotten.

During this first voyage, Ernest did not write any specific journals; however, he wrote letters home to both his wife and family. The letters expressed his realization of the dangers ahead and the possibility of never returning home. It was not only the German planes and U-boats that were feared by the crew but the especially brutal North Atlantic weather and exposure to heavy seas that threatened the ships. Winds howled day and night, and huge waves crashed over the bow. Lookouts and gunners suffered drenching cold rain. At times, the ship rolled and pitched, making it almost impossible to eat or sleep. The gut-wrenching fear of the vessel's rolling over was huge for men traveling during bad weather. Visibility was terrible during worsening weather, and collisions were frequent within the formation of ships. Some of the worst catastrophes of the North Atlantic were a result of vessels colliding while in convoy.[30] The rough conditions caused many types of damage in the unpredictable North Atlantic, including the loss of ships and crew from Ernest's convoy. Additionally, while working their shifts day and night, the Armed Guard rookie crew members suffered seasickness. While in a danger zone, gun crews remained at all times in the vicinity of the guns with meals served to them at their guns, day and night. The sickbay was not an available option on the merchant oil tanker. Ernest experienced all these fears for the first time on this convoy.[31]

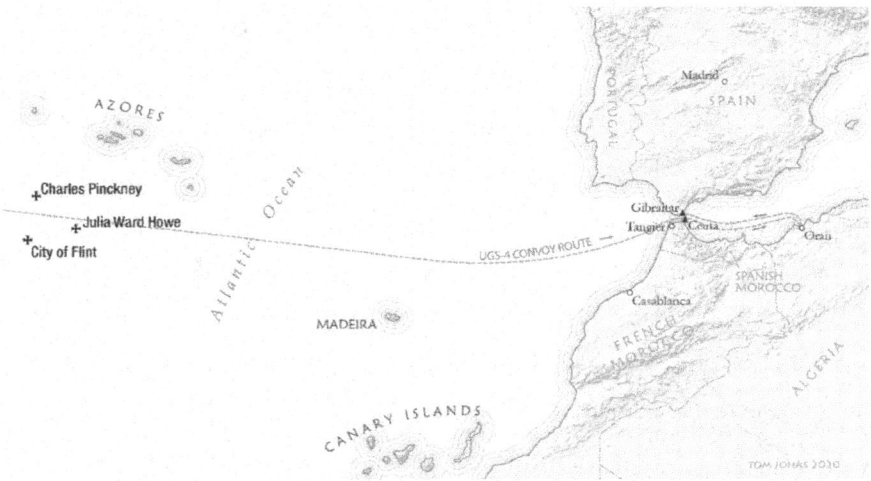

Figure 14. Convoy UGS-4, in a fleet of fifty ships and six escort destroyers, departed New York on January 13, 1943. Three ships, *Charles Pinckney, Julia Ward Howe,* and *City of Flint*, straggled from the convoy beginning on January 21 due to harsh weather conditions and were later torpedoed by U-boats and sunk. The *Esso Montpelier* safely arrived and delivered its cargo in Oran, Algeria, on February 3, 1943.

The oil tanker's Voyage Report provided the specific details of Convoy UGS-4, written by the Armed Guard commanding officer of the *Esso Montpelier*, Lt. James Thornhill. The report describes the various events encountered during the convoy's two-month voyage (January 13 to March 12, 1943), including the loss of three ships during its mission.[32]

UGS-4 Convoy left New York on January 13, 1943, at 0400 hours. The *Esso Montpelier* sailed in a convoy of fifty ships with an escort of six destroyers. The convoy headed for Oran, Algeria, just two months after the Allies landed in North Africa and took Algiers. Standard select winter clothing along with foul-weather clothing was issued to the Armed Guard unit of one officer and nineteen enlisted men in anticipation of the cold North Atlantic crossing. Nine new replacement Armed Guard personnel boarded the ship. (Appendix I (b) provides the original document from the office of the New York Port director, dated January 16, 1943, listing the names of Armed Guard personnel leaving the ship and those being newly assigned to it.)

The SS *Esso Montpelier*, a tanker and a US merchant vessel in time of war, sailed within the convoy at a speed of nine knots, loaded with fuel.

The Merchant Marine master and all officers carried out all instructions for Naval Transportation and US merchant vessels in time of war. On departure, the list of guns aboard the vessel included: one single-purpose 4"/50, one dual-purpose 3"/50; and eight 20 mm, located Aft, Forward, and Amidship. (Appendix I (c) is the original document from the Port Director's report for Arming Merchant Vessels, describing all gun types and details with their respective locations on the vessel.)

For the most part, the trip was uneventful, and the convoy had no contact with the enemy directly. Weather played more of a critical factor while en route. Three ships disappeared from the convoy on January 28: the *City of Flint,* the *Charles C. Pinckney,* and the *Julia Ward Howe.* The three American merchant ships, stragglers lost from UGS-4 due to extreme weather, never made it to their destinations with their cargo. They were all compromised and vulnerable due to rough weather and high waves, causing the ships' cargos to shift and partially sink the vessels. Convoys were often trailed by U-boats looking for "lame ducks"—ships that had dropped behind because of engine trouble or stragglers separated from the brood by fog or stormy weather, a frequent occurrence in the North Atlantic. The three stragglers from convoy UGS-4 had become targets, and ultimately these ships were torpedoed by German U-boats and sunk. Three different German U-boats—*U-575*, *U-514*, and *U-442*—claimed responsibility for the demise of these merchant ships. The losses included sixty-six lives and 19,316 tons of military cargo and supplies. U-boat log reports provided the time and locations for the sinking of the Allied ships. The number of lives and amount of military cargo lost were derived from Allied ship reports.

The *City of Flint* was torpedoed on January 25, 1943, by *U-575*. This cargo ship and its crew were recognized at the start of the war for their rescue of more than 200 survivors of the torpedoed British passenger liner *Athenia* on September 3, 1939. Fortunately, after the sinking of the *City of Flint*, the crew were rescued by a British ship and a Portuguese ship and taken to safety. Throughout the war, the courage of the men of the merchant ships was highly commendable. The crew of the *Charles C. Pinckney* battled *U-514* with exceptional tenacity and bravery, refusing to go down without a fight. In the end, they had the largest sacrifice of lives. The following documented reports provide accounts of the ships and the battles they bravely fought with the U-boats.

City of Flint[33]

The *City of Flint* sailed from New York as part of the convoy UGS-4. While en route, she encountered a storm that caused her deck load to shift, and she straggled from the convoy. The ship maintained a zig-zag course at 11 knots and tried to find the other ships when she was hit by one torpedo from *U-575* at 2205 on 25 Jan 1943. The torpedo struck on the port side at the #1 hold and ignited the oil and gasoline stored there. As the vessel settled by the head, flames engulfed the forward section. With the engines secured, the crew of ten officers, 30 crewmen, 24 armed guards (the ship was armed with one 4in, one 3in, and six 20mm guns) and one US Army Security officer abandoned ship with four lifeboats in rough seas within ten minutes. Then a second torpedo struck the port side aft of the bridge, and the ship sank bow first at 2305 about 300 miles south of Flores, Azores. Two crewmen and four armed guards died in the attack. The chief cook Robert Daigle was picked up by *U-575* as a prisoner and was later taken to a POW camp. Three of the boats stayed in the area for two days before setting sail for the Azores. They used a portable radio for sending distress calls. The following day, the Portuguese destroyer *Lima* (D 333) picked up 48 men and landed them at Ponta Del Garda, Azores. On 28 January, HMS *Quadrant* (G 11) (Lt Cdr. W.H. Farrington, RN) rescued the ten survivors in the fourth boat and landed them in Gibraltar.

Charles C. Pinckney[34]

On 21 Jan 1943, *Charles C. Pinckney* straggled from the convoy UGS-4 in heavy weather. Early on the 27 January, lookouts spotted a U-boat, the master changed the course, increased the ship's speed, and the armed guards fired at the U-boat (the ship was armed with one 4in, one 3in, and eight 20mm guns).

At 2043 hours on 27 January, *U-514* fired three torpedoes at the Liberty ship; a lookout spotted one of the torpedoes 750 yards away approaching the ship off the port bow. The master tried to evade, but one torpedo struck just abaft the stern [to the rear]. The explosion ignited a portion of the cargo; the blast blew the bow off forward of the #1 hold and created a pillar of flame that shot skyward. The engines were immediately secured, and most of the nine officers, 32 crewmen, 27 armed guards, and two US Army security officers abandoned ship in four lifeboats and one raft. A portion of the gun crew and the gunnery officer remained on board and opened fire at 2308 hours, as *U-514* surfaced 200 yards away. They claimed several hits and the sinking of the U-boat. However, the Germans made an emergency dive and escaped undamaged. The crew re-boarded the vessel, but the chief engineer discovered that he could not get steam up. At 2326 hours, a coup de grâce missed [shot from the U-boat] but a second fired at 0011 hours on 28 January hit, and all survivors abandoned ship a second time. The U-boat surfaced again, questioned the men in the lifeboats, and then left her victim in a sinking condition, which later sank over the bow.

The four lifeboats set sail, but during the night of 28 January, they became separated. On 8 February, the second mate, four men, and nine armed guards in one boat were picked up by the Swiss steam merchant *Caritas I* and landed at Horta, Fayal Island, Azores. The other three boats with eight officers, 28 men, 18 armed guards, and two passengers were never found.

Julia Ward Howe[35]

At 1807 hours on 27 Jan 1943, the *Julia Ward Howe* was torpedoed by *U-442* about 175 miles south of the Azores. The ship was a straggler from the convoy UGS-4 due to heavy weather. One torpedo struck on the starboard side between #3 hold and the deckhouse. The explosion blew off the #3 hatch cover, wrecked two lifeboats, and destroyed the radio equipment. The ship immediately took a 15° list but flooded slowly afterward and gradually righted herself on an even keel. Three shots from the aft 5in gun (the ship was also armed with one 3in and eight 20mm guns) were fired in the direction of the U-boat. The eight officers, 36 crewmen, 29 armed guards, and one passenger (US Army security officer) abandoned ship in two lifeboats and two rafts. The master, an armed guard, and the passenger were lost.

Forty minutes after the attack, a coup de grâce shot struck amid-ships and broke the ship in two. The U-boat then surfaced and questioned the crew, taking the second mate on board for closer examination. Later the mate was released, and the U-boat left.

The rafts were secured to the lifeboats, and they set sail for the Azores. After 15 hours, the survivors were picked up by the Portuguese destroyer *Lima* about 330 miles southwest of the Azores and landed at Ponta Delgada, but the chief engineer died of wounds on the rescue ship.

Convoy UGS-4 arrived at Oran, Algeria, on February 3. The *Esso Montpelier* successfully delivered its supply of oil in Oran. The convoy then left Oran at 1235 on February 12, arriving in Gibraltar on February 13 at 2030.

While the *Esso Montpelier* was docked in Gibraltar, as Second Mate John W. Bozarth reported, "A British corvette, about 200 feet long, was passing rapidly by us when she was hit by a torpedo." It was also reported that a second English destroyer was damaged by a torpedo when it went to the rescue.

The British corvette that was torpedoed next to the *Esso Montpelier* was Bryan's first wake-up call to the enemy below, one he would never forget. The proximity of that disaster was terrifying to the young sailor—graphic proof of the dangers lurking below the waves and threatening the cargo ships.

On February 22 at 0400, the *Esso Montpelier* left Gibraltar in a convoy of seventeen ships. Convoy UGS-4 finished their tour, as Lt. Thornhill reported: "On February 23rd the small fleet joined a convoy of approximately thirty-five ships from Casablanca. The entire convoy of fifty-two ships arrived in New York at 1900 on March 12, 1943."

CHAPTER FIVE

Early Years: Wilhelm Franken in Germany and at War

"The pre-condition of success is, in addition to an aggressive spirit, a capacity for making quick decisions, initiative, tenacious endurance, and unfailing skill!"

-U-Boat Commander's Handbook 1939-1942

W ilhelm Franken was born in Schildesche-Bielefeld in North Rhine–Westphalia (sixty-two miles northeast of Cologne), Germany, on September 11, 1914. He grew up with his older brother Ernst and younger sister Marie on the northern edge of a range of low forested hills called the Teutoburg Forest. The area was rich with myths and legends of battles and heroes of Germany's ancient history.

At the time of Wilhelm's birth, his father, Hector August Franken, was an officer in World War I from 1914 to 1918. After the war, Wilhelm's father returned home and became head of the middle school in Brackwede, which Wilhelm attended. Both his father and his mother Wilhelmine provided their children with a sound education and a strong Christian upbringing. Wilhelm transferred to Helmholtz-Oberrealschule in Bielefeld and completed his secondary school education. Upon graduation and after passing the Latin exam, Wilhelm chose to become a medical doctor.

Meanwhile, the global impact of America's Great Depression greatly affected Europe and was a contributing factor to dire economic conditions in Germany, Poland, and Austria. One in five of the population was unemployed, and industrial output fell by over 40 percent, causing widespread unemployment and starvation. In early 1932, unemployment had reached 25 percent, affecting families across Germany, including those in Wilhelm's town of Bielefeld. With his parents' support for continuing education, he left his family and childhood home and moved 220 miles north to Kiel, Germany, to study medicine.

Wilhelm Franken did not follow a typical medical school routine after he relocated in 1933 to Kiel University. Wilhelm began medical studies at the university, and the new surroundings soon proved much more interesting than medicine. Military service was not in his career plan. However, the unique maritime culture of Kiel could not be ignored. His routine included daily walks past boats, ships, and a large U-boat base. Hitler had become chancellor in 1933, marking a crucial turning point for Germany and, ultimately, for the world. Located in northern Germany on the southwestern shore of the Baltic Sea, Kiel was the headquarters for the German *Reichsmarine* (Imperial Navy) until 1935 and then became known as the *Kriegsmarine* (War Navy). As a result, Kiel became home for Germany's reestablished U-boat command.[36] Wilhelm's childhood memories of war heroes and legends were soon replaced with new stories from the bustling naval center at Kiel. Germany was, in fact, rearming. U-boats and warships were under rapid construction at the Reich's shipbuilding center. Hitler would lead one of the greatest expansions of industrial production and civil improvement Germany had ever seen.

Figure 15. Wilhelm Franken attended medical school at Kiel University in 1933. Kiel harbor was headquarters for the German Kriegsmarine (Navy).

After just one year, Wilhelm ended medical studies and began Navy infantry boot-camp training on the island of Dünholm near Stralsund, along the German coast of the Baltic Sea. Physically and mentally grueling, the first phase of training was a two-month basic infantry course, where military customs and courtesies, close-order drill, weapons, marksmanship, and tactics were taught. The officer candidates then attended sail training, learning the principles of general seamanship, standing watch, small-craft handling, meteorology, and celestial navigation while serving for three months aboard a three-masted sailing vessel in the Baltic Sea. Franken continued his instruction for an additional nine months as a midshipman overseas on a cruiser. After successful completion, he received an appointment to become a cadet at the German Naval Academy. He attended Mürwik Naval School, an academy for all German Navy officers. Mürwik replaced the German Imperial Naval Academy in Kiel and is a part of Germany's northernmost city, Flensburg, sixty miles north of Kiel. Wilhelm graduated in April 1935, joined the Kriegsmarine as a midshipman at the age of twenty-one, and was soon promoted to a lieutenant junior grade. He served as watch officer aboard several ships, acquiring the skills necessary before eventually taking command of his own U-boat.

After the outbreak of war four years later, Franken served as a gunnery officer with the Danube Flotilla—the first operational U-boat command created on September 27, 1935, under the command of *Fregattenkapitän* (Frigate Captain) Karl Dönitz. While serving under Dönitz, Franken was influenced by his strong leadership and personality. "The Navy represents the cream of the Armed Forces," claimed Karl Dönitz in later years. "And the U-boat arm represents the cream of the Navy." In 1940, after Franken had served for a year on the battleship *Scharnhorst*—the first German battleship with torpedoes—he was "hooked" and transferred to the U-boat command in Kiel where he attended Ship Artillery School. The U-boat service attracted strong personalities; men who had a hard time fitting into the rigid structure of the surface fleet often found U-boats a better fit. Franken felt that he was,

no doubt, better suited for undersea warfare. He served as a first watch officer on *U-331* under KptLt. Tiesenhausen for his first three U-Boat patrols
and participated in the sinking of the British battleship HMS *Barham* on
November 25, 1941.[37] Franken was soon promoted to a first lieutenant and
received the Iron Cross in recognition of his bravery during the missions and
enemy engagements aboard *U-331*.

U-Boats became the primary focus of Franken's military career. In
January 1942, he completed a commander-in-training course at the 24th
(Training) Flotilla in Memel, Prussia, Germany.[38] In March, as a newly
promoted *kapitänleutnant* (lieutenant), Franken took command of his first
crew of thirty-five men on board the submarine *U-565*. Unlike its predeces-
sor, the *U-565*—type VIIC, commissioned in 1940—was equipped with a
new active sonar device. Additional space was needed to accommodate the
device. The hull was further lengthened two feet immediately fore and aft
of the periscope, extending to an overall length of 67.10 meters (220 feet, 2
inches) and height of 9.60 meters (31 feet, 6 inches). Franken's disciplined
approach and years of education and training would soon be tested in his
first U-boat command.

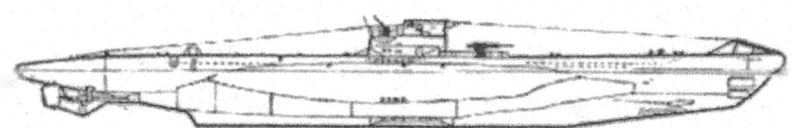

Figure 16. The VIIC U-boat, a capable fighting machine, had a test depth of 230
meters (750 feet). Its armament consisted of five torpedo tubes (four bow, one stern)
and fourteen torpedoes, an 88-mm deck gun (220 rounds), and a C/30 AA gun.[39]

The *U-boat Commander's Handbook* was the "bible" for U-boat commanders, and KptLt. Franken knew the book by heart. After all, it was written
by veteran submariners. The book gave precise instructions for the life and
death struggles ahead. "He who wants to be victorious on the sea must always

attack!" was one lesson that he would not forget. However, knowledge of defensive tactics against Allied warships was also critical for survival. The U-boat was weak in defense, and its best tactic was to remain undetected and use the element of surprise during torpedo attacks. To spot the enemy and at the same time avoid detection when lying just below the surface, the periscope should not have been raised until the submarine was well below the surface. It was the raised periscope on the surface that created the typical submarine silhouette and made it susceptible to hostile attack. During daylight, the sun reflection instantly gave away the location of the submarine. U-boat commanders were warned to dive early to avoid being seen when approaching enemy ships. In every situation, both on approach and in the attack, the submarine was to be guided by the motto: "He who sees first has won!"[40]

One important task that the U-boat faced when sighting enemy convoys was first to report the sighting immediately before attacking in order that other submarines in the vicinity could attack as well. It could then attempt repeated attacks. Avoiding detection was a priority. It was necessary to use both basic and advanced stealth tactics. If the U-boat was temporarily forced to submerge, it needed to press on in the direction of the general course of the convoy and renew the attack. U-boats needed the protection of darkness in order to escape on the surface. Therefore, during daytime attacks, the U-boat had to dive deep and leave the scene at full speed to avoid detection and retaliation by the destroyer escorts and neighboring ships. The greater the depth, the better the chance the enemy would have incorrect asdic (sonar) readings that could identify the U-boat's location. Remaining evasive was critical for the U-boat's successful escape from any Allied warship search pattern.[41]

For KptLt. Franken, it was time to put his military training to the test. His life and his crew's safety would depend on how well he would apply his skills at the moment of contact with the enemy. His childhood memories of battles and heroes were always on his mind. Franken understood that these were new times when new heroes and new battles would become history. His childhood dreams were now within reach and about to be tested at sea.

On April 11, 1942, KptLt. Franken and the crew of *U-565* departed La Spezia, Italy, on his first twenty-day U-boat patrol as commander. La Spezia, home of the 29th U-Boat Flotilla, was one of the leading military harbors in northern Italy. Their boats patrolled mainly in the Mediterranean Sea against convoys. U-boats usually carried four officers: the commander, an engineer, and two watch officers. On April 23, less than two weeks on patrol, Franken and his crew successfully torpedoed and sank their first ship, the British merchant freighter, *Kirkland*. This attack on convoy TA-36 (Tobruk to Alexandria route) was about thirty-five miles east-northeast of Sidi Barrani, off the Egyptian coastline. One crew member of the *Kirkland* was lost. The master, fifteen crew members, and six gunners were rescued. This sinking was an incredible success for Franken and his crew's first patrol: first torpedo strike and first sinking.[42]

U-565 returned to port at the naval base in Salamis, Greece, on April 30, and the crew celebrated their victory. At the time, Salamis was occupied by Germans and used as a naval port, including U-boat operations. Seven days later on May 7, after replenishing their supplies, *U-565* departed on their second patrol, which would last thirty-five days with the final destination of La Spezia. The patrol was uneventful, and they did not find any targets. It would not be until the sixth patrol that they would once again have success. In the meantime, Franken would focus on his personal life.

After docking in La Spezia on June 10, following his second patrol, Franken, at age twenty-eight, married the love of his life while on a thirty-day leave. The ceremony was held in Bremen on June 19, 1942. Waltraut Schomburg was the youngest daughter of the prominent pastor of St. Remberti Church in Bremen. She was very aware of the wartime dangers her family faced. Very likely, their ceremony was performed by her father, Pastor Walther Schomburg.

Franken and Waltraut would endure many separations when he returned to his U-Boat command. On June 25 and 26, within a week of their marriage, the British Royal Air Force and US Army Air Corps mounted a strategic bombing raid. The term "thousand-bomber raid" was used to describe three nighttime bombing raids against German cities, including Bremen, in the summer of 1942. They targeted railroads, shipyards, aircraft factories, and oil refineries, destroying and damaging homes with significant loss of life and injuries. Fortunately, Franken's new wife and family were not injured. Lifetime scars of war were in the making for both Wilhelm and Waltraut. They lived apart for long periods during the war with only their letters to keep each other informed. They would continue to see each other whenever possible during these difficult years.

CHAPTER SIX

Evasive Measures...Crash Dive

"The essence of submarine warfare is the offensive!

He who wants to be victorious on the sea must always attack!"

–U-boat Commander's Handbook 1939-1942

I t was not until December 18, 1942, and *U-565*'s sixth patrol in the western Mediterranean Sea off Algeria that KptLt. Franken sank his second ship. *U-565* torpedoed the British destroyer HMS *Partridge* while it was on an anti-submarine sweep. Thirty-eight men died. Another destroyer rescued the remaining 173 survivors.[43] Upon completion of the forty-day patrol, *U-565* returned safely to La Spezia. Franken and his seasoned crew now had a total of 157 days at sea with two torpedo hits and two sinkings.

Figure 17. *U-565* (while based in La Spezia, Italy) was a type VIIC boat, known as the workhorse of the German U-boat fleet, with twenty-one-miles-per-hour surface speed and ten-miles-per-hour submerged speed. They were commissioned in 1940 and were key to German naval operations in the Atlantic and Mediterranean.

The early dramatic successes of the 1942 German U-boat campaign in the North Atlantic and the Mediterranean began to change in 1943. Improvements in anti-submarine technology—such as radar, sonar, weapons, and long-range aircraft—reduced the U-boats' abilities to outmaneuver

Allied ships. Overall, the German Kriegsmarine now had close to two hundred operational U-boats. However, the arrival of more Liberty ships and improved Allied technology was turning the tide and resulting in more supplies reaching the war zone. Also, the cracking of the Enigma cipher, used by Germany for secure communication transmissions, was instrumental in giving the Allies the locations of U-boats.

The German Navy communication between headquarters and U-boat traffic was critical, keeping U-boats advised of approaching convoys within their vicinity. The Enigma machine used by German intelligence during World War II transmitted coded messages to U-boats and battlefields and relayed diplomatic communications. From a technical perspective, although the words are used interchangeably, the Enigma machine generated a cipher, not a code. A cipher system makes a word or message secret by changing or rearranging the letters in the message. A code replaces whole words or phrases with symbols. The Enigma machine allowed for billions of ways to encrypt a message, making it impossible for other nations to crack the German messages. However, in 1940, Allied code breakers at Bletchley Park, Milton Keynes, England, succeeded in reading the cipher text, and, in 1941, the capture of several German vessels provided key information in cracking the cipher encryption scheme. In March 1941, the German trawler *Krebs* was captured off Norway, complete with two Enigma machines and the naval Enigma settings list for the previous month.[44] Another capture on May 9, 1941, of *U-110* and their Enigma cipher machine, which was about the size of a typewriter, provided additional critical decryption information. The Allies were able to gather evidence of the planned invasion of Greece and also learned of Italian naval battle plans. The Allies also gained an advantage in North Africa by deciphering the secret messages of plans used by General Rommel's Afrika Corps. These high-level German sources were codenamed ULTRA. In February 1942, the German Navy became suspicious, believed that Enigma had been cracked, and changed the machine, increasing its complexity.

Throughout 1942, the Allied intelligence experts struggled to break the advanced Enigma machine and its new secrets. During that year, Allied losses in the Atlantic again increased alarmingly. It was not until December 1942 that the British finally broke this advanced cipher that they called "Shark" and the Germans called "Triton." The Allies could now discover where U-boats were hunting and could direct their ships away from danger. Overall, U-boat successes decreased significantly.

Under heightened pressure, the *U-565* crew prepared for their next combat patrol scheduled to depart on February 14, 1943. The U-boat remained dry-docked at La Spezia for servicing beginning January 2 with onboard work duties being performed by the crew. The U-boat preparations included offloading torpedo ammunition and provisions, gear servicing, cleaning, and training. A sea trial was finally scheduled on February 10, including radio direction-finder calibration and the completion of loading provisions of oxygen and torpedoes. Once medical examinations were finished and Franken's guidance to the crew had been provided, the final gunnery exercises and drills were performed. On February 14, 1943, at 1530 hours, KptLt. Franken wrote in his logs:

> Cast off La Spezia for the seventh patrol. Mission: Warfare in the western Mediterranean. Multiple crash dives for training, depth A-40 meters (131 feet)—repairs made to air intake head valve and no further issues. On Feb 16, more crash dives due to aircraft overhead. At 1638 hours, five well-placed aircraft bombs over the boat—the usual minor failures to depth gages, water-level gages, and light bulbs.
>
> Additionally, the bearing block for the transmission rod [periscope] magnification change mechanism is broken. The same damage occurred on earlier war patrol from aircraft bomb effect and was provisionally corrected by onboard means. At 2135

hours, repairs to the starboard diesel. The diesel failed. Will continue on one diesel.

On February 12, while *U-565* was undergoing maintenance and repairs, the *Esso Montpelier* was discharging cargo in Gibraltar and waiting for a return convoy to form near Casablanca. Their encounter with *U-565* would not occur until *Esso Montpelier* returned to the Mediterranean in April 1943. Until that time, KptLt. Franken and his crew hunted for other Allied targets.

KptLt. Franken, now at the height of his U-boat career, had become a skilled U-boat commander. His reports provided patrol and attack details. However, the first nine days of their seventh patrol began with multiple mechanical problems and repairs. Also, several days of storms and strong current, running in a northeast direction, slowed their progress. Numerous crash dives due to aircraft detection remained an ongoing issue throughout their mission. During this time, no one suspected that the Enigma code had been compromised.

Finally, on February 24, Franken surfaced at high speed along the coast of Algeria and north of Arzew Bay, twenty-five miles from Oran. Visibility was excellent, and he sighted a reported convoy with a large steam cargo ship escorted by two armed patrol vessels. At 1322 hours, an airplane flew above the cargo ship. Aircraft, an ongoing threat, continually forced Franken's U-boat underwater. *U-565* dived and kept a watchful eye on the action above. Suddenly, the cargo ship turned hard to port and fired a flare. Shortly after that, the cargo ship began firing out to sea from its rear gun. Franken was not sure but believed this was a form of U-boat alarm for the convoy. Although he could not see the impacts, he plotted the firing and detonations with the sound locator. Franken was confident the warning could not possibly be for his U-boat, given his distance. The airplane he had sighted was another concern; however, if his U-boat had been sighted by the plane, he knew his submarine would already have been attacked. Franken commanded, "Action

Stations!" The convoy formation zigzagged toward his U-boat, and Franken strategically set his targets to ensure an excellent firing position. Zigzagging in convoys helped to confuse U-boats about the actual direction a convoy was heading. Each ship of each column would turn one after the other, making it difficult for U-boats to formulate reasonable plans of attack.[45]

It was virtually impossible to define the length of a reasonable shooting distance, making accuracy very difficult for U-boat commanders. Franken could see the convoy guards: one fast escort vessel and one slow patrol guard (of the fishing trawler variety) set to the starboard side. The escort boat zigzagged at high speed back and forth in front of the steamer. The guard followed starboard, astern of the ship, both in strong protective positions. The U-boat commander recognized and described the "steamer" as a modern motor ship with one chimney (smokestack) and three masts—two fore and one aft. The "Maier Bug" style ship was designed with its V-shaped bulkhead, sizeable top surface, and a full cargo area. Franken observed the cargo ship's rear guns and anti-aircraft guns, painted gray, and the American flag. He estimated the vessel weight (based on the vessel size in terms of gross registered tons) to be 8,000 tons. Tension grew as Franken sensed the danger of the high-speed passes of the escort, which was only now 200 meters (600 feet) from his U-boat.

Additionally, with the calm flat sea and the airplane patrolling above, the periscope could only be raised slightly and very carefully. Observation, therefore, was challenging. To further add to the tension, "a fuse broke in the periscope, and it malfunctioned—now of all times!" The logs clearly showed Franken's frustration, as observations were now even more difficult. At 1354 hours, the American steamer slowly moved into an ideal target position. Franken then quickly turned hard rudder onto an attack course. *U-565* fired three torpedoes, one each out of Tubes I, II, and IV. He purposely chose a narrow scatter angle of 3 degrees, to increase the number of hits at a safe distance. He set his torpedo depth at 3 meters (9 feet, 10 inches) as the steamer was clearly traveling in ballast and sitting high, hence little-to-no cargo. Timely detonation calculations were critical considering the distance.

At the moment of firing, the other escort ship passed 600 meters away and forced Franken to lower his periscope, and he missed watching his target being hit. Two hits occurred at thirty-one and thirty-three seconds following their 480-meter run. The steamer stopped. Franken took his U-boat down, dived to maximum depth, touched bottom, and sat on the ocean floor quietly listening. After twenty-five minutes, he could hear heavy sinking noises and the sound of a bulkhead breaking. Franken and his men felt successful. He knew that both of the escort vessels were likely occupied for the time being with taking on survivors from the steamer. However, once they had rescued the survivors, the two escort warships would no doubt again begin actively searching for *U-565*.

As expected, the enemy's "listening and depth charge pursuit" for *U-565* began at 1426 hours. The escort warships began with sonar echoes and dropping depth charges. A third ship had joined in the hunt with S-gear (sonar), recognized by the irregular intervals and the sounds of the loud bangs. Franken described in his report the new S-gear equipment that had already been observed on his previous trip and mentioned in a radio message from BdU on February 11. About two and a half hours later, at 1655 hours, the depth charges and sonar pings ceased. The escort warships slowly moved north.

In total, Franken counted twenty-five depth charges, of which none were close to his U-boat. The escort ships had anticipated the U-boat escape route would be to the north. However, Franken had shifted course to the 150-meter depth line toward the east. Franken continued moving east, playing it safe, and did not surface to confirm his hit. At 2355 hours, Franken sent a radio message to U-Boat Command, informing them that he had sunk an American 8,000-ton steamer protected by two patrol vessels. He had successfully achieved this with two hits. *U-565* now received their confirmation from headquarters. The plane Franken had seen earlier at 1322 hours had been German. At that time during battle, Franken did not know of the aerial torpedo dropped by the German aircraft shortly after his hits. He believed the ship had been sunk by his torpedo hits alone. Later reports stated otherwise.[46]

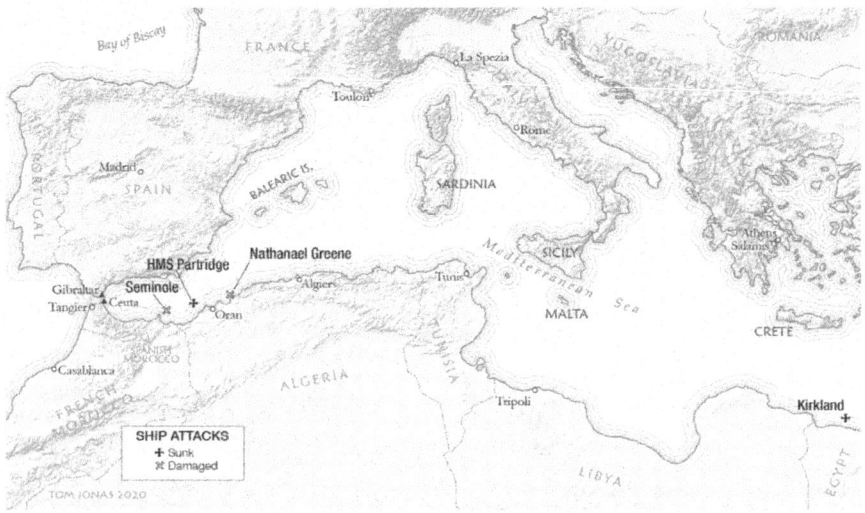

Figure 18. KptLt. Wilhelm Franken of *U-565*, while on his first patrol, sank the *Kirkland* off the Egyptian coastline in April 1942. In November 1942, on their sixth patrol, the submarine sank their second British ship, the HMS *Partridge*. While on their seventh patrol, *U-565* damaged two ships: an American, the *Nathanael Greene*, and a British, the *Seminole*.

The Allies' log report provided by the ship's master of the American Liberty ship, *Nathanael Greene*, also described the attack and provided the rescue details of the men and cargo, as well as the loss of the vessel. The torpedo attack by *U-565* had met its target, but the additional aerial torpedo by a German aircraft completed the ship's destruction. However, the ship did not sink according to the report.

> At 1354 hours, February 24, 1943, the *Nathanael Greene* in convoy MKS-8 was hit on the starboard side by two of three torpedoes, about 40 miles northeast of Oran. The first torpedo struck between the #1 and #2 hatches and the second in the engine

room. The explosions severely damaged the deck cargo, damaged the mid-ships deckhouse, disabled the engines, destroyed the starboard boiler, and flooded the forward compartments and the machinery spaces. One officer and three men on watch below were killed while seven others were injured. A few minutes later, German aircraft attacked the convoy, and the disabled *Nathanael Greene* was hit amidships by one aerial torpedo. Most of the nine officers, 32 crewmen and 16 armed guards (the ship was armed with one 4inch, one 3inch, and four .50cal guns) abandoned ship in two lifeboats, while 26 men jumped directly on to the HMS *Brixham*, which came alongside and later picked up the remaining survivors from the boats and the water. The minesweeper took the *Nathanael Greene* in tow until HMS *Restive* took over at 2100 hours and beached the vessel at Salamanda, four miles west of Mostaganem at 0630 hours the next day. The ship was declared a total loss, but USS *Redwing* managed to save at least 400 tons of her cargo.[47]

At early dawn the next day, February 25, *U-565* surfaced in northern Arzew Bay along the Algerian coast. The aircraft detection alarm sounded as two planes were visible in the periscope. *U-565* immediately dived seeking safety in deep water. Another radio transmission from U-boat Command at 2012 hours advised *U-565* that Italian agents had reported a convoy passing through Ceuta on a Mediterranean course. Franken set his course in the direction of the advancing convoy.

On February 26, after his search with repeated dives and surfacing on various courses along the North African coast, Franken observed a convoy under poor visibility conditions. Aircraft over the convoy were also sighted in the periscope numerous times on a western course; there were sounds of constant sonar coming from the same direction. By 1410 hours, poor visibility due to rain left only the sonar sounds for warnings. The volume of the sonar pings grew louder, indicating that the patrol vessel could not be far away. Franken ordered, "Action Stations!" As the sonar ping continued to increase, Franken was finally able to see four midsize steamers with three patrol vessels and an aircraft. They were traveling in a tight position near land at a distance of two miles and quickly moving out of sight. At 1610 hours, the *U-565* crew relaxed from their Action Stations, and the submarine returned to normal patrol status.

During the night, another radio message from U-boat Command advised of two more convoys, each traveling a different route. At 1815 hours, one convoy with twenty-one freighters, one tanker, two destroyers, and three corvettes had left Gibraltar on an eastern course into the Mediterranean. The second convoy was on a southwest course. Franken assessed his options and decided that operating in the vicinity of land at night and within the fifteen-mile zone (proximity within this land zone allowed for U-boat detection by enemy radar) increased the risk of being detected by sonar. He decided to pursue the eastbound convoy, pass it on the west of the island Habibas, and attack it during daylight.

The following day, February 27, at 0817 hours, north of Oran Bay, Franken observed a smoke trail in his periscope. Several steamers came into view. Above the band of vessels, he witnessed aircraft along with the convoy guards, corvettes, and three destroyers. At 0835 hours, Franken had his attack plan and headed toward the last steamer. Suddenly the convoy, which had previously been traveling in two or three columns, took an angular position and came in line alongside *U-565*. Franken instantly fired a torpedo from Tube II at two overlapping steamers. He managed to crash dive below just as a guard vessel and a corvette passed with loud propeller noises; thus, no hit confirmation took place. Franken raised his periscope again and observed a large tanker. On command, the crew fired three torpedoes out of Tubes I, II, and IV. Franken heard a hit after two minutes and two seconds. The destroyers, corvettes, and guards now knew his location. The U-boat dived again, rapidly varying course to avoid the advancing destroyers. Thirty-five well-placed depth charges were dropped by the convoy's escort vessels, but all missed their target.

By 1022 hours, running silent, Franken surfaced the U-boat to periscope depth. From a distance of 7,000 meters (4.35 miles), he observed a stopped steamer of 8,000 tons with a slight listing and a tanker of 10,000 tons slightly damaged. Franken's U-boat commander training advised reloading should be effected above water so as not to lose sight of the contact (target). The U-boat crew reloaded their torpedo tubes between approaches by escort vessels. For safety reasons, the reloading had to be interrupted several times because the escort vessels came too close, forcing *U-565* to dive. Once again surfaced, Franken observed the steamer making visible efforts to get underway, and, to Franken's disappointment, it was successful. The ship moved away at slow speed, protected by the escort vessel. However, the tanker remained. The destroyer was using sonar and zigzagged close to the large tanker. Franken decided to hold on for a finishing shot. He fired a torpedo at a solid angle shot of 180 degrees and a depth of four meters (thirteen feet). The torpedo hit its target after two minutes and five seconds. The sinking vessel slipped deeper with the bow still afloat. The quickly approaching destroyer forced Franken to dive to eighty meters while steering varied evasive courses. Twelve depth charges from the destroyer again missed their target. At 1408 hours, the destroyer's sonar signal became quiet. Franken, refusing to give up, returned to observe the status of the wounded tanker from 6,000 meters (3.72 miles). At periscope depth, he saw that the vessel was still listing, but the stern was now submerged in the water. The ship's bridge was entirely awash. Only the smokestack and the protruding bow were still visible. Franken felt the pressure to finish the attack and sink the ship.

At 1542 hours, Franken was determined to sink the tanker and moved into position for another attack. The destroyer was aware of the U-boat's approach and made a run toward them. Franken was prepared and ready to fire, held his position, and hoped for the best. He fired but missed his target and was forced to dive below and away from the oncoming destroyer. It was then too late to go deep enough to avoid the depth charges.

Franken, by now a veteran U-boat commander, strategically moved his U-boat *beneath* the listing tanker. He held his position sixty feet under the stricken ship, thereby avoiding any direct hits, as depth charges exploded around him. Once the destroyer moved away, Franken began taking various evasive maneuvers to avoid discovery. By 1710 hours, the sonar and depth charges ended. In all, he counted fifteen depth charges. The destroyer remained in the vicinity until 1830 hours. At 1842 hours, again at periscope depth, Franken could no longer see the destroyer or the tanker. Although the observation of the tanker's sinking did not occur, Franken believed it was likely, given that the increasing sea swells probably aided sinking. He sent a radio message to FdU:

> 0910 hours, one steamer 8,000 tons torpedoed, one tanker 10,000 tons–one hit, one coup de grâce. Left sinking due to depth charge pursuit. Still three bow, one stern torpedo. -Franken.

Ultimately, this proved not to be the case, verified by later reports about the British tanker. Although crippled, both ships were salvaged and repaired. Unfortunately, there was a total of five deaths[48]

The log report for the USS *Seminole,* traveling in Convoy TE-16, provided the details of damage to the ship.

British Tanker Torpedo damage by *Uboat-565* on Feb. 27, 1943

At 0910 hours on Feb. 27, 1943, U-Boat fired a spread of three torpedoes at the convoy TE-16 and heard one hit after 2 minutes 2 seconds, but could not observe the result due to the escorts. Due to her highly flammable cargo, the crew of fifty-one men immediately abandoned ship and were quickly picked up by a rescue ship in their convoy. At 1112 hours, the U-boat fired a coup de grâce at the damaged tanker and saw a hit in the stern, but the *Seminole* en route to Algiers, with 8,000 tons of aviation spirit, remained afloat and was salvaged and repaired.[49]

At 2127 hours, Franken received a radio message from FdU Italien (Italy) and reset his course towards a reported westbound convoy with a daytime attack plotted. The following day on March 1, north of Algeria, the *U-565* crew targeted one of the westbound convoy vessels, a destroyer, but missed due to an incorrect estimation of distance and speed. Franken sent a radio message to FdU requesting a return to La Spezia. Upon receiving orders for *U-565* to return to base, he reported on March 5 in his log report:

> Although the sea state is only 5 [moderate waves of 6.6 ft.], seas are so short and forceful, that a lookout on the bridge was struck so strongly against the bridge cladding, that he broke his upper arm. An Emergency bandage applied.

U-565 docked at La Spezia after twenty days at sea. For Franken and his crew, the patrol had not been easy, beset with many complications. Aircraft and sonar besieged the entire patrol, slowing their progress and limiting opportunities for success. Despite the difficulties, *U-565*'s success was fully recognized by the BdU as completing a very well-executed patrol and was credited with sinking two vessels and one torpedoed freighter. (Appendix II provides the original recognition comments from the FdU and BdU for *U-565*.)

CHAPTER SEVEN

Times of Courage

"Courage is resistance to fear, mastery of fear, not absence of fear."

-Mark Twain

M eanwhile, across the Atlantic, convoy UGS-4 returned from the Mediterranean to New York on March 12, 1943, after nineteen days at sea. Bryan's next convoy assignment, UGS-7, was scheduled to depart New York on April 1, 1943, leaving only twenty days for the *Esso Montpelier* to refit, fuel up, and take on barrels of fuel cargo.

Figure 19. Bryan while visiting Vera at her mother's home after he completed his Navy boot-camp training. Bryan always carried this photo with him on his convoys while serving as an Armed Guard on merchant ships in 1943.

During his liberty, Bryan's wife Vera joined him in New York. Their short visit allowed catching up on news of home, family, and their now four-year-old daughter, Linda. Bryan shared stories of his voyage events, crew ship living, and daily activities.

The hazards of his first convoy—heavy weather and constant danger—had already begun to test him. The realization of significant danger ahead had started to sink in. The young sailor felt distant from Vera and tried to close the gap in the short time before departure. While spending wonderful moments with her, he also felt the heartbreak of possibly never seeing his family again. Saying goodbye was much harder than before.

Bryan's nerves were forever being tested—tightening, releasing, and healing. Fear of the unknown inflicted stress in short amounts of time. The effect and duration of time of this level of stress vary with every individual. The lasting effects can be as little as a few hours or take days, weeks, or longer. For the second time in his life, Ernest Bryan would experience the heavy pressure of war. His fears and strengths would surface, ultimately affecting how he would handle himself under the extreme demands of the second high-risk journey he was about to undertake. Bryan felt very uneasy as he prepared for his ship's departure—and with good reason. Bryan's second convoy would once again travel into the dense German U-boat hunting grounds.

Figure 20. Bryan while visiting at home in with his three-year-old daughter Linda in Miami, Florida, before leaving for Armed Guard training.

On Bryan's first convoy, UGS-4, in January, he was well aware of the dangers of rough seas. Rough seas had caused three ships to capsize when their cargo shifted during heavy storms. The stragglers, no longer under convoy protection, then became easy targets and were torpedoed by U-boats. He also clearly understood the battle protocol and instruction for the commanding officer and crew of the merchant ships if engaged in battle: "There shall be no surrender and no abandoning ship, so long as the guns can be fought… The Navy Department considers that as long as there remains a chance to save the ship, the Armed Guard shall remain thereon and take every opportunity that may present itself to destroy the submarine."[50] If the merchant ship was at risk to fall into enemy hands, then the vessel had to be scuttled.

The secretary of the Navy issued instructions to the *Esso Montpelier* for scuttling merchant ships:

1) It is the policy of the United States Government that no US flag merchant ship be permitted to fall into the hands of the enemy.

2) The ship shall be defended by her armament, by maneuver, and by every available means as long as possible. When, in the judgment of the Master, capture is inevitable, he shall scuttle the ship. Provision should be made to open sea valves and to flood holds and compartments adjacent to machinery spaces, start numerous fires and employ any additional measures available to ensure certain scuttling of the vessel.

3) In case the Master is relieved of command of his ship, he shall transfer this letter to his successor, and obtain a receipt for it.

Either way, the ending would not be pleasant for the crew. Given the stress of operating aboard a civilian ship, men of the Armed Guard generally were regarded as "stepchildren" by the Navy. Even with all the on-board-ship experiences, being in the Armed Guard could be considered a "dead end" as far as a Navy career was concerned. The Armed Guard became known as the least desired duty in the Navy. The stakes were high, the recognition low, and the rewards few for the crews of merchant ship convoys. Still, the Armed Guard continued to protect the valuable cargo and diligently served their assigned ships and their Merchant Marine shipmates.

With one convoy under his belt, Bryan now had a much better understanding of the dangers ahead. Their oil tanker—along with troopships and munition ships—was still the real prize for U-boats on the hunt.

His appreciation of the hazards added to his apprehensions about the convoy. Before leaving New York, Bryan had written home to his father. Enoch shared the letter with his sister Bernice, the wife of Stacy B. Fountain, who in turn submitted the letter to her local newspaper. It was published on May 7, 1943, in the local newspaper of Chinquapin, North Carolina.[51]

April 29, 1943

Dear Sir

I am enclosing a letter written to my brother, who now lives in Miami, Florida, by his son, who is in the Navy. I am sending it for publication if you like. It at least shows that war doesn't kill our boy's deeper feelings and make animals of them as some people claim.

It is a copy of a letter written by Coxswain Ernest Bryan of Miami, Fla., serving in the US Navy, somewhere in the Atlantic, to his father, a former Onslowan, E.W. Bryan, of Miami, Florida.

Yours truly,

Mrs. Stacy B. Fountain (Bernice Bryan)

Hello Dad,

Gee, but it seems like a long time since I saw you last. I sure would like to see you again and know that you are happy. I never realized before just what you meant to me until I came in the Navy and was sent so far away from you. Being so far apart has brought you so close to me, and now I know just how much you mean to me.

You know something; your sailor son is mighty proud of his Dad and mighty proud that he is your son. I want to say right now that I wish you all the luck and happiness in the world and I sure hope after my next trip I can go home and be with you for a while even if it isn't for very long. Don't worry about writing Dad, because just as long as I get a card or a letter from you once in a while and I know you are thinking of me, then everything is all right by me.

I will be so glad once this war is over and your sons and all the other folks' sons can go home to stay. Then I don't know how to act. The sailor of the family is tired, Dad, tired of going to sea, and tired of looking at guns and ships being sunk, and boys losing their lives when by rights should be planning a life for themselves and their children. I am proud to be serving my country and my people and proud to be fighting for what is right, but I pray to God this will end soon and that there will never again be a time when we will have to take up arms against our fellowmen. Sometimes I wish I were dead, so I wouldn't have to see fathers and mothers and sons and daughters' heartbroken over the loss of one of their dear ones, but when I think about it, I see how foolish I am because after all, someone has to face it, and maybe by my being here it is giving some other guy a chance for a little rest and happiness.

Having Vera up here with me has certainly given me a little relaxation and peace of mind. After seeing her and being with her, I am ready and willing to go anywhere anytime they want to send me. My only regret is in not getting to see my daughter and you and the rest of the family and friends.

I would like to ask a favor of you and my brothers, Dad, in case I don't come back some time, kinda see that Vera and Linda are all right and that they don't ever have to go wanting. Please do it for me, will you? Thanks

Well Dad, guess I'd better close now, so until you hear from me again, give my love to all and I will always be your loving son.

Ernest

Both the Allies and Axis were in a powerful position in the North Atlantic at the beginning of 1943. However, the U-boat attacks and ships sunk did not peak until March in both the Atlantic and Mediterranean. Many factors were significant, but the new ULTRA intelligence was critical as far as United States involvement was concerned. U-boat traffic's enciphered messages could now be read within hours of their dispatch. Additionally, the increase in US ship production, aircraft coverage, and improved technologies outweighed the substantial loss of American merchant ships caused by the U-boats. The tide was beginning to shift in favor of the Allies.

During the same period that Bryan was writing home to his father, KptLt. Franken was also writing home. While still docked in La Spezia, preparing for *U-565*'s eighth patrol, Franken wrote a personal letter to his wife or a family member to lessen their worries, stating:

Onboard - 3.4.[3 April] 1943—"I have a strong sense of danger."

—Wilhelm Franken

I have been commander now for one year, a long and eventful time. From a rookie to an old ferryman, and soon, my time is here served. The boat is docked again at the pier. The crew brings each of their last belongings on board. Others stand around and clap. On the outside, we are quiet with our thoughts. It is followed again by weeks full of concentration and tension. In a few weeks, we will be back. We hope, with success, but undoubtedly healthy and well.

I am not so arrogant that I believe nothing can happen to me. The opposite is the case. I have a strong sense of danger. I fought hard for my tonnage. I have had bad luck many times. However, success was always on my side when the boat was in danger. That is why I hope that luck will stay with me during those times.

You are worried again, and I cannot relieve you from your worries. You do not know enough about how things run down here, but from a purely logical point of view, it has little use. Because when you think I'm in danger, I am fully ok and when you think I am safe, I am in danger. So stay in peace and confidence, and believe in my skills. Such trust helps and strengthens.

I take luck as a precious gift, without becoming overbearing or reckless, and if it ever leaves me, it doesn't mean that everything is lost. Then I can prove that I am as brave as my brothers. I am sad that you cannot meet my crew. If you would get to know them and realize how my men think of me, I believe you wouldn't be worried at all.

Now don't worry and wait in peace until you receive the message in a few weeks that *U-565* and Franken have returned fit and healthy. Acquire the "Wiener Illustrierte" from March 31st and the magazine "das Signal" Nr. 7. You can find pictures of my boat in both of them.[52]

Franken and crew departed on patrol seven days after convoy UGS-7 departed New York harbor.

CHAPTER EIGHT

Convoy UGS-7 Underway

"The Merchant Navy, with Allied comrades, night and day, in weather fair or foul, faced not only the ordinary perils on the sea but the sudden assaults of war from beneath the waters or from the sky."

–Winston Churchill, the dark days of 1941

B efore the departure of Convoy UGS-7 from the Port of New York, thirteen Armed Guards of the *Esso Montpelier* were replaced by twenty new Armed Guards. Ernest Bryan remained on board the tanker for his second convoy duty, which consisted of seventy-two Allied merchant ships and nine escorts.[53] The convoy departed on April 1, 1943, heading across the North Atlantic towards the Mediterranean Sea. (Appendix III provides the ship names and destinations of the ships traveling in convoy UGS-7.)

As expected with security requirements, the *Esso Montpelier* master provided limited information to the crew on their destination. They first traveled south and then northward towards the North Atlantic. "Loose Lips Might Sink Ships" was a standard wartime poster and a critical protocol for sailors. Although he was unsure, Bryan believed the tanker's destination was North Africa. The convoy would eventually pass through the Straits of Gibraltar, the bottleneck for all ships entering the Mediterranean. The Straits themselves were a dangerous part of the journey. They are very narrow and were always heavily patrolled by Allied vessels. U-boats also hunted in these waters, and U-boat commanders were on constant heightened alert for Allied matériel, men, and fuel headed to North Africa.[54]

On this convoy, Bryan wrote letters to his wife in the form of daily journals, covering the personal events of his voyage. The first entry of Bryan's journal did not begin until April 11, 1943. This particular day was significant, given that Bryan recognized firsthand and expressed concerns over the threat of German U-boat attacks. He recorded in his journal, "We have had two submarine alarms so far." The underlying danger began to slowly seep into his written journals and letters with overt fears of not returning home.

He made no mention in his journal about the first lost ship from convoy UGS-7, very possibly due to the "loose lips" protocol. The American merchant ship *James W. Denver* was torpedoed and sunk on April 11. The vessel, a new Liberty ship loaded with 7,200 tons of cargo (sugar, acid, flour, aircraft parts, vehicles, bulldozers, and twelve P-38 Lockheed aircraft on deck), had strayed off course from the convoy on their maiden voyage due to heavy fog and overheated engine bearings. As a result, it fell behind and was torpedoed by *U-195*. All crewmembers (forty-two merchant seamen, one passenger, and twenty-five Armed Guards) abandoned ship and set sail in lifeboats for the coast of Africa.[55]

Later stories told by the surviving lifeboat crew of engineers, stewards, and Armed Guard gunners provided details of their encounter with the U-boat that had sunk their ship with two torpedoes. On the third night after the sinking, a vague shape was sighted in the dusk, and someone yelled, "Destroyer dead ahead!" To attract attention, they switched on their life jacket lights. Almost before they realized what was happening, a submarine appeared directly across their course. The lifeboat grated against the hull, and a German officer shouted at them from the conning tower, "Where are you from?" One of the crew responded, "Brooklyn!" The German laughed. "That's where the baseball comes from," he said in good English. A German sailor handed them a carton of cigarettes. From the bridge, the officer shouted a course for them to steer, and the U-boat moved off into the night.[56] The incident was a very fortunate encounter.

Whether Bryan knew about the loss of the *James W. Denver* or not, the submarine detection and resulting battle alarms began having their effect on his and the other crewmen's nerves—much like a time bomb ticking with ever-increasing tension and pressure.

The crew's main outlet was writing letters and talking of home within the confines of their off-duty bunk time. According to World War II Postmaster General of the United States (1942-1945) Frank C. Walker, "It is almost impossible to overstress the importance of mail. It is so essential to morale almost on a level with munitions and food."[57] Writing letters home was a regular and essential pastime while at sea, particularly on Bryan's sleepless nights. His wife and family were always at the front of his mind, not knowing if he would see them again. Strict censorship governed the letters servicemen sent home from overseas, and the men sometimes chafed under its restrictions. But they also censored themselves, careful to keep from worrying their loved ones back home. For the men on board merchant ships, mail was sent and received to and from overseas designated distribution centers and once their convoy returned home to their US port.

Bryan wrote the first of his daily journals for his wife while his convoy was heading into U-boat infested waters.

Somewhere on the North Atlantic

April 11, 1943

To my darling wife, Vera,

I suppose I should have started this quite a long time ago, but now that I have, I will attempt to keep as close an account of this trip as possible. This is our eleventh day at sea, and so far, everything is going along fine; our destination is still as yet unknown. We are certain of discharging our cargo somewhere in North Africa.

We have had two submarine alarms so far, and I am tickled pink with the way my boys' man their guns. Nearly all of them are green, and I can truthfully say they are catching on fast. I have taken all nine of my progress tests for Boatswain, and my average on them is 3.5. I have also taken my final exam and passed it with a mark of 3.16. As soon as I get back to the States and can get to the Armed Guard Center, I will take my exam from them. I pray that they will see fit to give me my rating. The Ensign said he was positive I would get it with the recommendation he gives me. I sure do hope so. Vera, the weather is beautiful out here, and my only regret is not having you with me.

The sky is as blue as Linda's eyes, and the sea is like a big blue carpet that stretches for endless miles in every direction. At night (I know it is dangerous, but I have to marvel at it), the moon is a ball of pure silver, and the ships stretch out for quite a way all around us with the white surf curling up under their forefoot. It really is beautiful.

Well, I guess I had better go to chow now, and I will resume this tomorrow night if the ship is still afloat.

Bryan wrote about the weather he encountered. It ranged from stormy to mild. At times this allowed him to sleep topside. The oil tanker quarters were cramped below with air thick and foul like a submarine. It was considered heaven to stand up on deck and breathe in the fresh air whenever the weather was calm. The weather was very different on this tour of duty than during his first mission in the North Atlantic.

April 12, 1943

Somewhere on the Atlantic

Last night was calm and peaceful, with the exception of a pretty stiff breeze blowing from the bow. I have been sleeping outside for the last couple of nights, and it almost blew me out of my bunk last night. I forgot to mention that there was a burial three days ago; we couldn't get any information as of who it was. It kinda makes you feel funny to know that some poor guy who was looking forward to going home at the end of this trip is now at rest at the bottom.[58]

We have had a very peaceful day, and I hope the night is the same. Honey, the phonograph is playing "There Are Such Things." And believe me, it sure makes me feel awfully lonesome and lost without you, I love you so much. Well, I have to go on dusk watch in just a little while so being as there is not anything else to say, I will close until to-morrow evening.

From April 15 to 19, Bryan began to include more of his military duties and concerns. The dangerous nature of the mission was taking its toll, and he expressed it more often the closer the convoy moved towards its destination.

We picked up our first plane escort today late in the afternoon, so I guess we are in pretty close. The weather is still just about the same, but it is a little cooler now. I finished my inventory of ammunition today and also changed half of my armor-piercing shells for anti-aircraft shells that will give quite a few more cracks at any of the lousy heinies [Germans] they send over. From the reports, we are really going to have a nice reception waiting for us. What the hell, we can give them a thing or two to think about if they don't get too lucky on the first egg [bomb] they drop at us. The destroyers we have with us had a little work-out this morning when we had a sub alarm. Believe me, these babies are really the business when they cut loose. Well, that just about winds this day and last night up. We are only a couple of days from Oran now, so everything will be ready for the boys to get paid when we get in. I fixed the range and Scal [sight] dial on my big anti-aircraft gun, so it is ready to tear loose. Picked up our limey [British] escort of Corvettes this noon, and our escort took part in the convoy into Casablanca. We should arrive in the Mediterranean tonight or tomorrow.

April 19, Passed the Rock of Gibraltar around nine o'clock this morning. I mounted the sights on all 20mm guns today, am now ready for the planes. Bad news tonight, it looks as if we are going to Malta. The Captain thinks so too. Well, if we do, I hope we can at least deliver our cargo so it can do some good over here, even if we don't get back ourselves.

The merchant ship's master, Captain Lionel E. Crowder, was concerned along with Bryan about the potential for a Malta route. It was well founded. Since 1940, the Siege of Malta had been a raging battle between the Allied and Axis air and naval forces for control of the Mediterranean. The fight for the strategically important island, then a British colony, pitted the air forces and navies of Italy and Germany against the Royal Air Force and the Royal Navy between 1940 and 1942. From Malta, the Allies could attack Axis supply lines to North Africa. Without this strategic Allied checkpoint, Rommel, the German commander of North Africa, would be able to march unchecked into Egypt, the Suez Canal, and the Middle East. For the Allies, this would have been catastrophic. Churchill demanded Malta be held "at all costs." It would be a treacherous journey to Malta, the most heavily bombed island in World War II. Towns and facilities were bombed, as well as ships in transit and in the harbor. The convoys bound for Malta suffered substantial losses of ships and crew. The Siege of Malta was still underway, and the last air raid over Malta took place on July 20, 1943.[59] Fortunately, for both the ship's Captain Crowder and Bryan, destination orders for Malta did not occur.

Wartime instructions, relative to US armed merchant vessels, gave the Armed Guard officer or petty officer exclusive control over the military functions of the Armed Guard crew. In addition, he held responsibility for the execution and detailed reporting of all the US Navy regulations under which a vessel functioned. The commanding officer of the Armed Guard was the military advisor and represented the Navy Department for the ship's master. The civilian master commanded the merchant vessel and was charged with safe navigation and the safety of all persons on board.[60] Armed Guard Commanding Officer Ensign Elwyn Middleton, USNR, wrote the Armed Guard log reports for *Esso Montpelier* during convoy UGS-7. The reports provided specific interesting details surrounding its voyage within the convoy.

Voyage Report of *Esso Montpelier* April 1–April 19, 1943-Outbound

We departed from New York, the USA, at 0942 hours on April 1, 1943, on the SS (Steam Ship) *Esso Montpelier*, a vessel of 7,698 gross tons, owned by the Standard Oil Co., of New Jersey and chartered to the War Shipping Administration. In the gun crew were 24 gunners, two Signal Men, and one Radioman.

Our cargo consisted of 80,000 barrels of Naval fuel oil, nine Lockheed P-38 Lightning Aircraft, large cargo boxes of aircraft accessories, and the forward hold full of spare gas tanks. The planes and cargo boxes of aircraft accessories were in the forward hold and full of spare gas tanks. The planes and cargo boxes were carried on the deck on special stands built for that purpose.

A heavy fog made the run to the convoy rendezvous very difficult. It was necessary to use the whistle fog signal throughout the whole day. At 1700 hours, we reached the convoy rendezvous. The fog did not lift until 1300 hours on April 2. In the meantime, the ships had to stay together by means of the fog whistle signals. At 1700 on April 2, we were in our proper place in the convoy, which was position 42.

On April 3, three more ships joined the convoy, making a total of 42 ships (according to my count). The escort consisted of eight American Destroyers, and the speed of the convoy was 9-10 knots. The *Esso Montpelier* is capable of making 11.5 knots.

At the first opportunity to fire the guns, which was April 5, we fired three rounds on the 3inch -50 Caliber and three short bursts on each of the 8-20mm's. The 4inch -50 Caliber [standard low-angle, quick-firing deck gun used for anti-aircraft protection] was not fired because there was no safe direction in which to fire due to our position in convoy. During the night of April 5, one Patrol Bomber plane came over the convoy and flashed its lights.

At 1545 hours on April 6, the Commodore signaled enemy Subs were in the vicinity and ordered that the guns be manned. Battle stations were taken immediately by the crew and maintained until 1630 hours. No Subs appeared, but the watch was doubled until 2100 hours. At 2030 hours, one vessel showed two red lights and dropped out of the convoy but joined us again the next day. Three days later, a Seaman 1/c fell against a ventilator on the boat deck aft and hit his head, causing a jagged wound about one inch long on the left side of his head. The wound was dressed and has healed satisfactorily.

A signal from the Commodore on April 11 at 1030 hours said that there were enemy Subs in the vicinity and ordered the guns manned. The general alarm was given, and the men stayed at their battle stations until secured at 1145 hours. No Subs appeared. The Captain thought that he heard two depth charges, but I did not hear anything. An unidentified freighter passed on our port side at 1100 hours on April 13.

Again, on April 15, we had a signal from the Commodore that enemy Subs were in the vicinity and for all ships to man their guns. Guns were manned at 0950 hours, but a rain squall came up at 1015 hours, and the signal was hauled down on the Commodore's ship. The guns were secured upon the signal being hauled down. On the same day, two Destroyers about three points on our port bow fired several rounds of ammunition with surface guns apparently carrying out the battle practice. Late in the afternoon, one Patrol plane circled the convoy. It was the first plane seen on the eastern side of the Atlantic.

The following day, April 16, two planes in the forenoon, two in the afternoon and one in the early evening, circled over the convoy. They appeared to be British Flying Boats. Planes (usually one at a time) were overhead the greater part of the day and early evening on April 17.

We were met at approximately 0930 hours on April 18 by seven (my count) English corvettes. At 1130 hours, Section 3 of the Convoy and 8 American Destroyers, which had escorted the convoy from the Port of Departure, separated from us. We changed course at the same time, leaving them to go on their way. There were thirty-two ships (my count) left with us, including the Commodore and the Vice-Commodore, escorted by the seven English corvettes. Planes, usually one at a time, circled over us all day. At 1800 hours, the Convoy was rearranged so that we took up an outside position, being position twelve. The number of men on watch on the exposed side of the vessel was increased.

Land was sighted at approximately 0630 hours on the morning of April 19, which proved to be Cape Spartel [Morocco at the entrance of the Straits of Gibraltar]. We proceeded through the Straits of Gibraltar and were joined at approximately 1000 hours by several ships from Gibraltar. At least two of the ships were French and carried troops. The Straits were cleared at 1115 hours when we entered the Mediterranean.

- Ensign Elwyn Middleton

Until this time, business was as usual for Bryan: completing the inventory, shoring up the ammunition for the ship's forward guns, mounting the sights on the 20 mm guns, and changing armor-piercing shells for the anti-aircraft arms. Early Monday morning on April 19, the remaining ships of Convoy UGS-7 left the North Atlantic and moved into the Mediterranean, passing by the Rock of Gibraltar. The only information Bryan knew at this point was that they might be headed to Malta to drop the ship's cargo. According to Bryan, Captain Crowder was "feeling uneasy."

Figure 21. A convoy cargo vessel, crossing the Atlantic at dusk.

That evening, there was a full moon, and to pass the time, Bryan and some of the other crew members played poker while off duty. Bryan managed to net himself winnings of ninety cents. He slept a few hours in an uneasy fitful sleep. His thoughts once again were consumed with concern about not returning home. He journaled of his love for his wife and daughter and wrote a poem that he enclosed with his letter.

Ships

I like to watch the moon on high sending down its rays of light
and see the stars way up high like diamonds shining in the sky.
Then look out at the ocean so beautifully cold and dark.
And watch the ships floating by like some tiny bit of bark.

On such a great big ocean, it seems they might get lost,
but then I see the buoys flashing like some guiding ghost.
They sail the ocean over to all the seven seas
and then come sailing safely home to people such as we.

In the early dawn of April 20, as the ship passed Oran, more of the convoy split away, headed to other locations, but the *Esso Montpelier* continued to Algiers. Several other vessels had joined convoy UGS-7 while passing through Gibraltar. A couple of the new ships had taken positions next to the *Esso Montpelier* sometime during the night.

At 0750 hours, Bryan's uneasy feelings and premonitions of danger were validated in the worst way when an enormous explosion woke him. Alarms were blaring, and the off-duty ship's crew sleeping below scrambled from their bunks, racing topside to their battle stations. With fear and anxious anticipation, Bryan reached the top deck, unsure if their ship was in trouble. A second explosion blasted through the morning air. Smoke and flames were shooting up on the ship's starboard side. Bryan quickly assessed the nature of the damage and smoke. Without the sounds of airplanes above, Bryan knew enemy torpedoes were to blame. Convoy UGS-7 was under attack!

CHAPTER NINE

The Stalking of Convoy UGS-7

"Gefechtsstationen!" (Action Stations!)

-KptLt. Wilhelm Franken, *U-565*, April 19, 1943

Ten days earlier, on the morning of April 8, 1943, *U-565* had left La Spezia once again on her eighth patrol. On Franken's previous patrol, although he had torpedoed and damaged two ships—the *Nathanael Greene* and the *Seminole*—he had been unable to sink his targets. On this patrol, his military success would require a more aggressive approach in dealing with the enemy if he wanted to ensure success in destroying his targets. The strategy "Hit hard and fast, using the element of surprise, and then make a rapid retreat" was tested, and lessons were learned. These were great lessons from his *U-boat Commander's Handbook*. However, he had also learned that "power is not revealed just by striking hard and often but… by striking true" (Honoré de Balzac, 1850). Franken would take his tactics further if given another opportunity.

Franken's patrol orders directed *U-565* westbound in the Mediterranean Sea. During the first four days after leaving La Spezia, his U-boat was tracked daily by Allied aircraft, forcing ongoing crash dives after surfacing. On April 13, Franken reported "stationary locating gear [radar equipment] when passing south of the Balearic Islands [190 miles east of Spain's coastline]." That night, *U-565* dived again due to land-based locating radar near the Habibas Islands off the Algerian coast, northwest of Oran. He wrote in his log report, "With bright as day moonshine, coordination of the land-based gear [radar equipment] with aircraft or fast boats is likely." Franken continued westbound, and, on April 18, four more crash dives were required following surfacing. FdU instructed *U-565* to extend its attack area to the east. A radio message from BdU on April 19 advised all, "West Boats: From Agent report [Convoy] passed Ceuta about 1200 hours course for the Mediterranean."

South of Spain, Franken surfaced at 2141 hours. The reported convoy was in sight at a range of 10,000 meters (6.21 miles).

Franken wrote in his logbooks:

At the front, escort vessels, among them a large destroyer, which zig-zags at high speed in large legs ahead of the formation. Escort's radar in use. To Action Stations!

I was forced off by the escorting destroyer—steered evasion courses. In the very good visibility—it is the full moon night, lightly cloudy—there is no prospect of getting into shooting position. So as not to waste time unnecessarily, because the convoy runs at 10 knots and I can also be detected at any time by the radar, I decide to refrain from further attempts at attack and to run ahead to attack submerged in the early morning twilight. …With a 2-hour lead, I am always able to reach a favorable shooting position with the help of the listening gear.

At 0445 hours before dawn on April 20, 1943, *U-565* surfaced, scouted the area, and prepared to dive below. KptLt. Franken thoroughly checked the small wave swell and weather conditions, observing excellent visibility. Winds were at a gentle to moderate breeze. The sea swells were low and light, both conditions favorable for making an attack. He knew he would only have one chance to hit the desired targets by surprise. The prize for his success would be the recognition he was hoping for as a U-boat commander.

Defensive maneuvers were essential in KptLt. Franken's strategy when engaging the convoy. Once his torpedoes reached their targets, evasive tactics would be critical to help ensure his crew's survival. Most importantly, he needed to not merely damage his targets but successfully sink them. Precision was imperative. The sonar reading of the convoy was at 45 degrees when *U-565* dived. His earlier calculations had been correct. He knew the group of ships could not go more southerly due to the proximity of the coast, and it would not divert to the north for reasons of saving time. He also knew the rate of speed for the convoy, and this gave him a two-hour lead to get to an advantageous battle position.

At 0630 hours at his strategic position ahead of the convoy, Franken ordered, "To Action Stations!" The convoy was not yet visible, but the sonar return continued to grow louder. The U-boat crew quickly prepared for action, and Franken knew that by early morning light the oncoming convoy would be in sight. Time ticked by slowly for the crew, who were ready and waiting.

At 0723 hours, the convoy came into view about sixty miles west of Oran. Heightened anticipation and tension spread among the crew while they waited for the order to fire. Depth charges continued as the convoy moved through the water at medium speed and on a course of 50 degrees. Franken waited for the lead destroyer group to pass. The crew held total silence. A sigh of relief escaped from all once the destroyers passed over their U-boat. *U-565* had not been detected! Once the enemy escort passed, the U-boat commander knew he had to surface again quickly to observe the enemy and not lose valuable time.

Franken noted the convoy traveling in three columns and that the most valuable steamers were in the center. He now put all his attention on the middle row, the highly protected center. Quickly focusing, Franken began searching for a clear shot at multiple valuable targets. He maneuvered the U-boat closer toward the middle row and reached their ideal shooting position. With the torpedo set to four meters depth (fourteen feet), Franken issued the "Los!" (Fire!) command. Tube I torpedo launched for a distance of 400 meters at the right position of 95 degrees. Franken hit the first target in the stern after fifteen seconds and 200 meters; it was a loaded 6,000-ton freighter (later identified as the *Michigan)*. The freighter's aft rudder cabin flew upward through the air, as did its lifeboats and various other parts of the ship. Ammunition stowed in the aft cargo hold exploded one after another in small, ongoing detonations.

The freighter *Michigan* immediately stopped dead in the water and began to sink. Franken quickly dived, moving to his next target without chancing visual confirmation of the damage. Depth charges detonated continuously one after another in small but progressively closer explosions. Using his periscope, Franken saw the second target of the convoy come into shooting position. Franken instantly decided to fire Tube II and Tube III at the troop transport, a two-stack passenger ship of at least 12,000 tons (later identified as the *Sidi-Bel-Abbes*). He believed the convoy commodore was on board because the ship had several flags flying. This vessel was a worthy target that the U-boat commander could not pass up. With a torpedo depth set to 7 meters, Franken fired at the ship at a range of 1,000 meters, firing angle 336 degrees with a scattering angle of 4 degrees. At such close range, the danger of being located by sonar increased, requiring traveling as slowly as possible and maintaining absolute silence. After thirty-one and thirty-three seconds respectively and a 500-meter distance run, the two strikes aimed at fore- and midship reached their targets. The second torpedo hit with a violent impact. At periscope depth, Franken saw the red glow of a fire, spurts of flame, and a black explosion column. He knew the ship could survive a massive explosion along its flank; however, a blast under the hull would snap its spine and usually result in the ship's breaking into two pieces and sinking within minutes. In this case, the transport had been obliterated, and he saw the buckling mast and the transport heel over. He knew it was irretrievably lost. Success!

KptLt. Franken was now ready for the third ship. A large oil tanker (later identified as the *Esso Montpelier*) was positioned directly in his path. Franken instantly prepared for the firing of the Tube V torpedo. In that moment, Franken caught a glimpse of the oil tanker turning directly toward the U-boat's extended periscope, at a short distance of 300 meters, "exactly towards me." There was no choice; so as not to be rammed, he had to abandon the attack and go deep. To avoid a collision, Franken quickly took the submarine down to forty meters. The waters of the Mediterranean were known to be clear enough that anyone on the surface could easily make out the hulk of a U-boat at periscope depth. So, Franken was fine at forty meters down. The prized oil tanker had unknowingly been saved from destruction by Franken's planned torpedo!

Franken piloted *U-565* around the destroyed ships. He swiftly chose an escape path and positioned the U-boat beneath the previously targeted oil tanker. The commander's training kicked into high gear, and now his rapid escape required a straight course with limited zigzagging to avoid depth charges and the oncoming destroyers. He and his crew could hear loud sinking noises as the troop transport ship broke apart and small ongoing detonations from the torpedoed vessels. They had successfully destroyed not only the cargo ship *Michigan* but also the troop transport *Sidi-Bel-Abbes*.

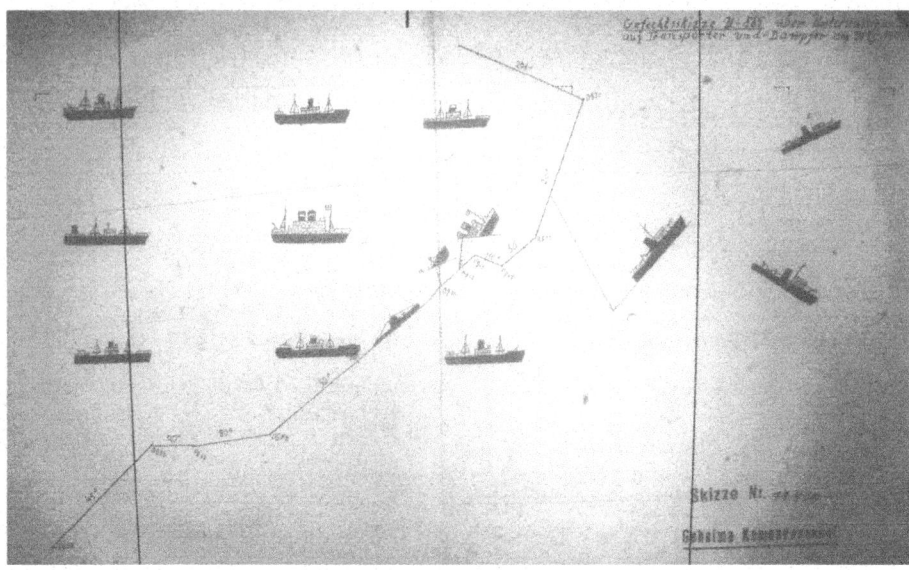

Figure 22. The *U-565* diary sketch was submitted with KptLt. Wilhelm Franken's patrol log report dated April 20, 1943. Shown is *U-565*, and the path it traveled while sinking two ships in convoy UGS-7. The third targeted ship, the oil tanker *Esso Montpelier,* is on the top row, the third ship from the left, based on Armed Guard Ernest Bryan's account of witnessing the sinking troopship *Sidi-Bel-Abbes* from the starboard side of his oil tanker.

At 0830 hours, Franken reported, "It has gotten lively among the convoy, and we are run at by a screening destroyer with sonar. The Destroyer ran over us at 20 degrees, and two corvettes remain in the vicinity." The extra protection provided by the screening destroyer and the two corvettes forced Franken to turn away from the convoy at full speed. He could not resume the attack from the outside and risk being detected. It would be better to get in a shot at the last ships of the convoy. Franken steered various evasive courses, running silent. By 0957 hours, intense sinking noises could still be heard, likely by the torpedoed steamer. After making his escape, it was 1055 hours, and even the smaller explosion sounds had stopped. (Appendix IV provides the translated original patrol report of KptLt. Franken for *U-565*.)

The destruction of the two ships that had been torpedoed by *U-565* resulted in many lost lives. However, the quick decision by KptLt. Franken to abort the release of the Tube V torpedo targeted for the oil tanker and to go deep to escape being rammed no doubt saved the lives of the men on the *Esso Montpelier*, as well as his own and those of his men on *U-565*. Bryan wrote in his journal later that night of his near encounter with the elusive *U-565*. The unseen German submarine that had caused so much death and destruction would be lodged in his memory forever.

April 20, 1943 Mediterranean

I was awakened at ten minutes of eight this morning by an explosion from a torpedo. The French troop ship "Sidi Bel Abbes" loaded with troops had been hit amidships, and it almost blew her in two. She sank in five or six minutes, and as far as we could learn, not very many got off. She was broad abeam of us on the starboard when she was hit! We have so far today, four alarms, and the last one, the convoy opened fire on a submarine that popped to the surface in the center of the convoy. It was just luck that she wasn't sunk because it turned out to be a friendly one. We have passed Oran with part of the convoy going in there and the rest of us we think will go to Algiers, from there I don't know. I love you darling and think of you all the time. —Ernest

(Appendix V provides a copy of Bryan's original handwritten journal of the attack.)

The sinking of the *Sidi-Bel-Abbes* was Bryan's firsthand torpedo casualty experience. Both he and his shipmate S1/c William Hollenback witnessed the *Sidi-Bel-Abbes* rapidly sinking just a few hundred meters away. In later years, both men spoke of their close encounter with mortality and the tragedy of the men who died on that day. Ernest and William remembered the towering flames and the heat felt on their faces. The troopship had only just joined the convoy in Gibraltar and had taken position next to the *Esso Montpellier* during the night. The fog and smoke were so heavy that, at first, Bryan was unsure exactly what had happened to the vessel. Wreckage and bodies covered the ocean. He heard men yelling for help as he took in the scene.

Bryan's most dreaded fear—of men aboard ship never returning home—entered his mind as he observed the carnage in the wake of the sinking ship that was destined for the bottom of the Mediterranean. With depth charges exploding around him, the young sailor knew a U-boat had struck and felt the terror of what was lurking below.

Abruptly, the *Esso Montpelier* shifted direction in a zigzag defensive maneuver. Bryan had little time to think about the emotions brewing inside him. His training kicked into action as he manned his battle station. In spite of the sinking of the troopship and death all around them, their ship continued to move through fog and smoke. Bryan knew his oil tanker would not attempt any rescues; the danger and risks were too great. The men in the water would have to wait for the rescue ships to pick them up.

The smell and sight of spreading oil were strong, and the whitecaps of the sea were no longer visible in this scene of a watery grave. Bryan could not describe his deepest feelings: fear, pain, and shock—all in an instant. The ticking time bomb of tightening nerves wound tighter than ever before. The unseen danger was still lurking somewhere beneath them. There were fleeting thoughts of his wife and daughter at home. Bryan and the other Armed Guard crew remained at their stations until 1100 hours, ready for whatever would come. Besides the French troopship *Sidi-Bel-Abbes*'s destruction, the crew members of convoy UGS-7 experienced four more alarms that day. Their nerves were raw and on edge, adrenaline racing.

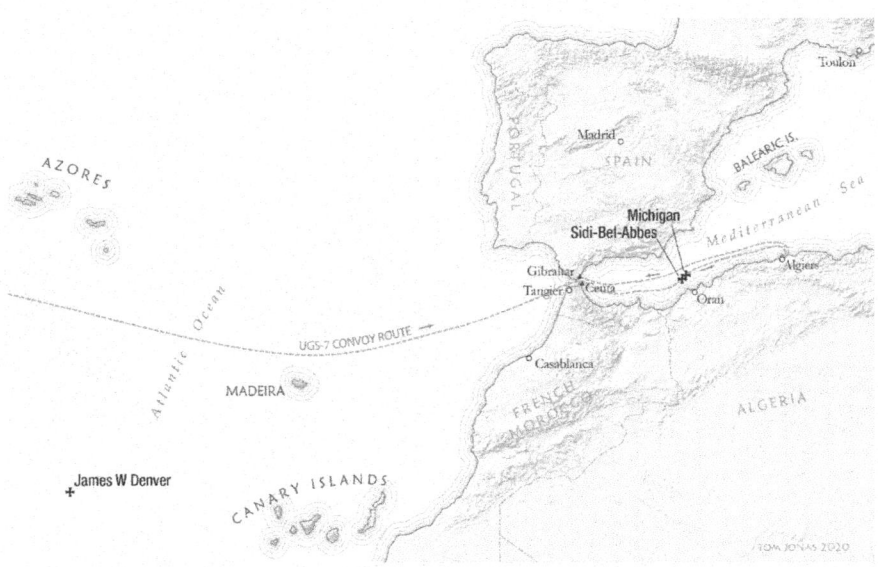

Figure 23. Route of convoy UGS-7 from New York to Algiers, showing the locations of the sinkings of three ships. The *James W. Denver* was torpedoed and sunk on April 11, 1943, after straggling and drifting from the convoy route because of engine trouble. After passing through the Straits of Gibraltar, the *Sidi-Bel-Abbes* and *Michigan* were both torpedoed and sunk on April 20, 1943, by *U-565*. The *Esso Montpelier* safely delivered its cargo to Algiers.

Bryan did not write in his journals or possibly was not aware at the time about the other sinking in the convoy, an American merchant cargo ship named *Michigan*. The loss of human lives was most significant with the French ship *Sidi-Bel-Abbes*, employed as a troopship for Senegalese infantry. The vessel carried 1,131 Senegalese soldiers. Bryan witnessed the loss of 611 soldiers, killed that fateful day. Many of the men died in the fire explosion while others drowned; however, there were also 520 men rescued. Luck would have it that the American merchant ship *Michigan*'s eight officers, twenty-nine crewmen, twenty-three Armed Guards, and one passenger all survived and were rescued. The American men in the *Michigan*'s lifeboats rescued many Senegalese men before being transferred to ships and taken to Oran. The British Royal Navy escort vessels, HMS *Foxtrot* and HMT *Stella Carina* picked up the survivors.

Figure 24. American Freighter *Michigan*.

On April 20, 1943, while the *Michigan* was preceding the *Sidi-Bel-Abbes* in convoy UGS-7, *U-565*'s first torpedo struck the freighter between the #1 and #2 holds with a muffled explosion. The blast caused extensive damage to the hull and minor damage to the deck and superstructure. Within two minutes, all eight officers, twenty-nine men, twenty-three Armed Guards, and one passenger escaped the ship in two lifeboats and three rafts. The damaged ship sank after an hour, plunging bow first. All 6,300 tons of military cargo and a deck load of Army gliders were lost.

Miraculously, Bryan and the *Esso Montpelier* had come out of this attack alive and intact, never knowing that they too were in *U-565*'s crosshairs. Bryan's later reflections on this tragedy were of tremendous sorrow, which every true seaman knows in his heart. He realized that many men had died that day and had taken the final plunge to their graves below, never to return home. He always believed that these men were the true heroes of war: the men who gave their lives for freedom.

Figure 25. French Troopship *Sidi-Bel-Abbes*

On April 20, 1943, while transporting a battalion of Senegalese troops, 50 tons of ammunition, and 542 tons of oil from Casablanca to Oran, the *Sidi-Bel-Abbes* was torpedoed forty miles west of Oran. The ammunition exploded violently, and the oil it was carrying caught fire, sinking the ship within two minutes. There were 611 lives lost and 520 saved.

After the April 20, 1943, attacks on UGS-7, Ensign Middleton wrote in his ship's log report of the assault, providing the additional details of the incident and the following alarm:

> Early morning, April 20, at 0755 hours, an explosion was heard immediately followed by a signal from the Commodore to man the guns. Guns were manned until 1100 hours. The explosion was seen by the Chief Mate and several of the gun crew. The witnesses said that there was one big sheet of flame about 4 or 5 columns over from us, broad on our starboard beam about where the French ship, *Sidi-Bel-Abbes,* had taken her position in the convoy when she joined us the night before at Gibraltar. The fog was so heavy that we could not determine what happened to the vessel. I was not sure that it was the French ship, but she

was the only one missing from the Convoy as far as we could tell. (I later learned that the *Sidi-Bel-Abbes* and *Michigan* were both lost that morning). At 1130 hours, a submarine was sighted on our starboard quarter, about 1-1/2 miles away from us. Several ships near the submarine opened fire on it. We immediately manned the guns but secured at 1155 hours after a signal from the Commodore that the submarine was friendly. No hits were made on the Sub. At 1230 hours, Section 1 of the Convoy separated from us and headed for Oran and Algiers. There were five British invasion barges to join us from Oran and 18 ships left in section 2 of the Convoy with six English corvettes as escorts. The Vice-Commodore became our Commodore. Friendly aircraft circled the convoy most of the day.

At 1930 hours, a Corvette on our port bow fired five rounds of anti-aircraft ammunition, and the Captain of the ship sounded the general alarm. We manned the guns immediately, but I believe that the Corvette was merely carrying out a battle practice. Smokescreens were laid by corvettes on both sides at the approach of dusk. At 2345 hours, one of the Navy lookouts saw a Corvette fire two red and one white flare into the air upon the approach of aircraft. He thought the aircraft was hostile and rang the general alarm. Guns were manned and secured immediately upon my learning what the alarm was sounded for. Depth charges went off at intervals throughout the night.

April 21, at 0630 hours, the general alarm was sounded upon the approach of hostile aircraft on our port bow about 3 miles away. A British anti-aircraft Cruiser had joined us in the night and opened fire on the planes (I saw only one) along with several ships on the port side of us. The plane did not approach any guns. At 0645 hours, an escort vessel on starboard quarter opened fire with anti-aircraft guns. I did not see any aircraft, but two gunners on the stern gun said they saw one plane which turned away upon being fired on. Smoke floats were put out at 0700 hours. At 0930 hours, the signal was received to reduce speed and form a single column in preparation to enter the port of Algiers, Algeria. At 1230 hours, a pilot came aboard and took us into the harbor. We moored alongside the oil tanker *Francunion VI* at 1330 hours and began to discharge the cargo into the *Francunion* and two barges that were brought up. The oil cargo was discharged by 1830 hours. -Ensign Elwyn Middleton

For Bryan and the crew, tensions remained high, following the U-boat attacks, enemy planes, and even the sighting of the friendly submarine. Sleepless nights and high tension continued throughout the convoy as the oil tanker headed towards its destination.

CHAPTER TEN

Delivering the Vital Cargo

"Your first task is to bring to port the cargoes vital for us at home or for our Armies abroad, and we trust your tenacity and resolve to see this stern task through. We are a seafaring race, and we understand the call of the sea..."

–Winston Churchill

"My nerves are shot all to hell this trip. I jump at the slightest noise, and sometimes I could scream my head off I get so nervous."

–Ernest Bryan

On April 23, after the oil cargo was discharged, sailing orders out of the Port of Algiers were given to the *Esso Montpelier* for the following morning at 0530 hours. Until that time, shore leave was granted. Algiers was the headquarters of Allied forces in North Africa. The city of Algiers lay in an arc of beaches and bluffs gradually rising to low hills ten miles inland parallel to the Mediterranean Sea coast. The crew was ecstatic to receive a much-needed release from the confinement of the ship's steel walls, even if only for a few hours.

Bryan wrote in his journal, "Cleaned up all guns—today got half of them painted and the other half ready for painting. I went ashore today and went to a show. I saw Deanna Durbin in *The Amazing Mrs. Holliday*. I also bought two souvenirs for my darling wife, but doubt she will like them."

Bryan's nerves were showing signs of strain as he and the crew anticipated a rumored air raid that night. Six British transport vessels, loaded with troops, had docked in port that day, and some of the British crew expected the enemy might attack. Adding to his worries, four of Bryan's crew members were not back yet from their shore leave. Bryan was relieved when they all returned safely and wrote, "Turned out to be a quiet night, and luckily the four missing crew returned in the morning. The Ensign will give them extra duty for being AWOL [Absent Without Leave]." The brief time of relaxation after going ashore quickly ended for the men over the anticipated air raid. The crew spent their evening writing letters and talking about family, as the Easter holiday quietly passed.

On April 24 at 0700 hours, the American oil tanker weighed anchor and moved out into the bay to join the convoy headed for Gibraltar and ultimately back to New York. The gun crew was mustered, and all hands were present. There was one alarm that day—the sound of torpedo strikes—but it was just depth charges set off by a corvette off the port beam. After the convoy passed Oran on April 25, they received an emergency order to reverse course and head back to Oran to pick up five more ships joining their convoy.

Bryan felt relieved that they would not remain long in the dangerous area of the Mediterranean where enemy aircraft and U-boats frequently attacked. On April 25, Bryan wrote in his journal, "My nerves are shot all to hell this trip. I jump at the slightest noise, and sometimes I could scream my head off I get so nervous." A roller coaster of emotions continued to consume the men as they went about their duties. Bryan completed painting the guns. His passion for order and cleanliness served his ship well. He would fret over the ship's guns, striving for perfection as he stocked the ammunition and worked on the gun assembly and sights. Bryan became an expert in each of the gun's mechanics. These were not chores to him; his assignment was pure passion.

The convoy arrived at Gibraltar on April 26 at 1700 hours and anchored near the entrance to the breakwater. For centuries, the narrow passage of eight miles between the Mediterranean and the Atlantic had been controlled by the British military from their naval base on Gibraltar. Thus, the British monitored virtually all naval traffic into and out of one of the world's most important shipping lanes. Gibraltar had been transformed into a fortress, commonly referred to as the "Rock," protecting this major sea route since the early 1700s. During World War I, Gibraltar served as an assembly point for ocean convoys, but that had been about the extent of its contribution to the war effort. During World War II, the British forces maintained the latest designs in heavy artillery there and expanded Gibraltar's airfield, and fighter planes and seaplanes based at the Rock soon made passage through the straits a risky proposition for U-boats. "Convoys assembled under Gibraltar's protection to carry vital supplies to British forces in North Africa. And the

November 8, 1942, Allied invasion of Vichy French North Africa—Operation Torch—was headquartered in Gibraltar."[61]

At 2200 hours, there was an air-raid alert, which proved to be a false alarm. At regular intervals throughout the night, small depth charges were fired by British patrol boats targeting U-boat activity.

On April 27, liberty was arranged for the members of the gun crew. However, nasty weather kept the men confined on board. Bryan wrote in his journal, "Depth charges continued to drop all night." To pass the time, Bryan played poker with his crew and wrote letters home. Whenever he had any spare time, he spent it studying for advancement, learning the mechanics of seamanship and the coxswain responsibilities. The challenge was huge. His on-the-job training allowed him to apply theory in the day-to-day operations of the ship. Day-and-night ship duties and never-ending false alarms made for sleepless nights, further wearing on crew morale and strength.

Finally, on April 29, Bryan was able to go ashore at Gibraltar with "his boys." One downside of crewing an oil tanker, unlike other ships, was that docking required berthing at oil installations, well away from town and city centers. And oil docks were excellent targets for enemy aircraft. The crew was jumpy, coursing with adrenaline. A much-needed night on the town and a break from the thoughts of war finally came to pass. The men made their way to town, looking for the closest bar.

William Hollenback, Bryan's oil tanker crewmate and Armed Guard gunner veteran, commented, "When on convoys and finally getting liberty after dropping our cargo, the first thing we would do was head for a bar in one of the strange countries. We would go in groups of four to five men since it wasn't safe to be off on your own." Bryan spoke of one of those nights with amusement. He and a few of his crewmates went to a bar and ordered drinks. The bar was crowded with Navy servicemen on liberty from the other ships at port. All the men were there for the same purpose: to have drinks and let off some steam. Bryan tells a story about the bar with a smile.

"A big fella came up to my barstool, grabbed me by the arm, and threw the first punch."

With that, the fight was on. "I got my butt kicked," Bryan says with a slap of his hand and a laugh. "A couple of my buddies jumped in to help me out. We all managed to get out of there, finally, in one piece."

After two more incidents of the same nature, Bryan says, "I was having a drink at the bar, minding my own business, and someone starts a fight with me again. Finally, one of my buddies tells me what was going on. One of the other guys in our crew would point me out to some big guy in the bar and tell him I had said he was as 'yellow as a chicken.' As soon as the fight broke out, this crew member would come to my aid, but I would not know that he had instigated the fight.

"This fun at my expense finally came to an end one night, and my crew buddy was at the receiving end of the next fight," Bryan said with a chuckle.

Bryan was lean and fit at five feet, eleven inches. Muscular in a medium-size frame, he could out eat many of the crew. He spoke fondly of the ship's cook, amazed by his cooking skills. Tanker conditions, for the most part, were considered better than freighters, and so was the food. According to Bryan, there was one perk to life on the ship—the food. Creamed chipped beef on toast, commonly referred to as "shit on a shingle," was one of Bryan's favorites. He would "have no problem downing second and third helpings if ever there were any leftovers."

The days in port passed slowly for the crew while completing their assignments: painting and gun repairs and ensuring that everything was in perfect working order. On April 30, still docked in the Gibraltar harbor, Bryan wrote in his journal, "Lots of Navy ships came in today, and I would bet they are getting ready to give Rommel a little bit of hell. Sure wish I was going with them! All the guns are painted now and hope to finish all of the turrets tomorrow. Had to give my big gun a going-over today to be ready for whatever is to come."

Bryan and his crewmates were aware of the massive ship activity around them and speculated that battle was forthcoming. General Erwin Rommel, Germany's field marshal in North Africa, was under siege. Fighting continued and ultimately forced the Axis surrender on May 13, 1943, as a result of British attacks from the east, Americans from the west, and Free French from the south. The Axis forces in North Africa, having sustained 40,000 casualties in Tunisia alone, surrendered; 267,000 German and Italian soldiers became prisoners of war. Rommel had been flown out to German-held territory in Europe before the surrender.[62]

Meanwhile, by May 8, Bryan and his crew members had become more anxious and impatient. New information was delivered to the crew by the merchant ship's Captain Crowder. Three ships—two British and one American Liberty ship called *Pat Harrison*—had been damaged near the Spanish Coast in Gibraltar Bay by "human torpedoes." That night, Bryan wrote in his journal to his wife Vera, "Three ships sunk inside here last night by human torpedoes. Maybe we will get it too if we do not leave here soon. I hope darling that you will always be waiting for me and wanting no one but me. Goodnight, my sweetheart, darling. I love you."

These "human torpedoes" were another undersea weapon used to assault merchant cargo ships, an easier target for the Italian Navy than dealing with the lethal British warships. The torpedo, also known as the Italian *maiale* (pig) due to its cumbersome steering, was launched from an old 5,000-ton Italian tanker, the *Olterra*. The *Olterra* had been scuttled by its crew at Algeciras, a port city on the Bay of Gibraltar on June 10, 1940. The ship was moored across the Bay of Gibraltar in a Spanish port only a mile away, allowing easy access to the port of Gibraltar. The harmless-looking scuttled ship had been secretly converted to launch torpedoes through a hatch cut six feet under the waterline of the vessel, acting as a secret base. Powered by its own propulsion system, the torpedo was straddled by a one- or two-man crew as if they were sitting on a horse. The "pig" slowly approached a target ship, and the crew magnetically attached Limpet mines (a type of naval mine), set to explode on the ship's hull. The charge could be set with a delay of up to two and a half hours, allowing the divers time to escape.[63] Three vessels, the American Liberty ship *Pat Harrison* (7,000 tons) and the British freighters *Mahsud* (7,500 tons) and *Camerata* (4,875 tons), were all targeted by the Italians on May 6. When the charges exploded, the American transport was heavily damaged, including one death, and the other two ships sank. The *Esso Montpelier* crew members, anchored at the port of Gibraltar during the enemy attack, were paid a port-attack bonus.[64]

Finally, on May 9 at 1745 hours, a signal was received over the radio to weigh anchor. At 1820 hours, the *Esso Montpelier* was underway with sixteen other ships from Gibraltar to join the New York-bound convoy from Algiers and Oran. The convoy was sighted as soon as they traveled into the Straits. The convoy temporarily preceded the *Esso Montpelier* through the Straits to the Atlantic, and, on May 10, the *Esso Montpelier* took up its permanent position in the convoy formation. There were approximately thirty ships in the convoy, escorted by seven British corvettes. At 1330 hours, three more ships joined the convoy from Casablanca along with seven American destroyers. The British escorts left the convoy to the American destroyers, as friendly planes circled overhead most of the day.

CHAPTER ELEVEN

Homeward Bound

"[Mariners] have written one of its most brilliant chapters. They have delivered the goods when and where needed in every theater of operations and across every ocean in the biggest, the most difficult and dangerous job ever undertaken. As time goes on, there will be greater public understanding of our merchant's fleet record during this war [World War II]."

-President Franklin D. Roosevelt

"In some cases, they [the men who operate merchant ships] run even greater risks than the boys in the regular army and navy. When we realize that, over and over again they land from one torpedoed ship, and as soon as they recover from wounds or exposure they start on another trip; we can hardly fail to pay homage of supreme courage."

–Eleanor Roosevelt

The convoy home was finally underway. Bryan was counting the days since the *Esso Montpelier* left the Rock of Gibraltar on May 9. The trip homeward once again required preparation for further attacks with firing practice, gun maintenance, and repairs. Bryan went up to the bridge, took the helm, and steered the massive ship for an hour and a half. In fact, he had several opportunities to take the helm of the 450-foot oil tanker. He studied daily so he could take his rating exam once they arrived in port. He spent time with his crew members—Koch, Kemm, and Pozzerto—helping them practice semaphore flags and Morse Code so they could pass their Seaman 1/c exams. Bryan expressed in his journal his need to stay busy: "Anything to pass the time and make the days go faster, thus bringing me a little closer home."

By May 15, the weather in the Atlantic became rough, which had the ship pitching and rolling. The convoy's commodore reported that a mine had been spotted. Bryan believed escort vessels might have handled and exploded the mine. To Bryan's disappointment, his training at the helm was less frequent. He continued his studying, assured by his ensign that he would get his rating with the ensign's recommendation. His penchant for orderliness and cleanliness was evident in his drive to wash down and paint all the quarters with his crew despite weather conditions. "If the sea is calm enough for us to be able to stand up, we work! When we get to New York, we should really get a good word from the inspectors because there have been a lot of changes since we left," Bryan proudly stated. The feeling of pride in a ship binds a man to navy life. Bryan felt the pride connection to this merchant oil tanker. By May 25, with weather delays, Bryan and crew completed the final cleanup and the painting of the ship's guns and turrets.

Figure 26. The 450-foot oil tanker SS *Esso Montpelier*, while undergoing heavy seas during a convoy voyage across the Atlantic Ocean.

Bryan wrote again in his journal, expressing his excitement about returning home to his wife:

Tuesday, May 25, 1943, Almost Home. Painted all guns today and they sure do look good. We should get a good mark on them. I have a lot of checking up to do in the morning cause I hope to go ashore after the mail tomorrow afternoon. I sure hope Linda's picture and a bunch of your letters are there for me. It sure has been a long time since I heard from you and I am really looking forward to your letters. Gee but it sure is nice to be coming back again to the good old USA. We will be inside N.Y. Harbor around 10:00 in the morning, and seeing that lady of liberty will sure look good. Well, honey, I am awfully tired so that I will close for now. Goodnight darling, I love you.

On the morning of May 26, all felt the excitement of safe arrival in New York harbor aboard the ship. Bryan wrote again to his beloved Vera:

Wednesday, May 26, 1943, Going inside (5 months aboard today).

Hello darling, our mail was brought out to us before we ever dropped the hook this morning, and you will never know how happy I was to read your letters. I have been ashore today to get paid and to pick up any other mail we had, but there were only two more letters. It doesn't look as if I will get leave this time! They say we have to have six months sea duty. I sure did and still do want to see you awfully bad. You see, darling, I need you too just as much as if not more than you need me. I love you, darling, and I am going to call you tomorrow so until then goodnight my honey. I love you. -Ernest.

One of Vera's two additional letters described a bad dream she had had about Bryan on April 20, the same day of the sinking of the ship that was torpedoed next to him. She would be overjoyed to find out that the incident in her vision had luckily turned out fine for him and the crew of his oil tanker.

Ensign Middleton provided his final report of convoy UGS-7, giving high praise for his Armed Guard crew and the merchant crew.

At 0700 hours on May 25, the Vice-Commodore and about 20 ships left the convoy and headed southeast. We arrived in the Port of New York on May 26.

Relations with the officers and men of the merchant crew were pleasant and satisfactory. They co-operated with us in every way possible in defense of the ship and rendered many favors and extended many courtesies beyond their lawful obligations to the gun crew.

I cannot praise too highly the spirit of willingness to work and fight which prevailed among the gun crew. They took great pride in keeping the Ordnance Materiel in good condition, and their quarters clean. They stood good watches and responded enthusiastically to each general alarm. At all times, their morale was high, and I believe they would have given a good account of themselves in action had they been called upon to do so.

–signed Ensign Middleton

New orders were received, and Ernest Bryan would have but a few days of leave before departing on the next convoy, once again aboard the *Esso Montpelier*. Ensign Middleton and few of his Armed Guard crew would also continue on this convoy with him. Bryan's crewmate William Hollenback was given different orders for his next convoy and left the *Esso Montpelier*.

While in New York, Bryan was able to take his rating exam, which he passed, achieving his official promotion with a coxswain rating. His spirits lifted with this achievement, and he called home to update his wife and family and to express his disappointment in not having any leave to visit with them. His remaining time at the dock was spent preparing for his next convoy that was heading somewhere towards the iceberg-laden waters of the North Atlantic. Seamen who served on merchant ships throughout the war claimed the North Atlantic was the worst ocean they ever traveled. The new convoy, HX-242, would be Bryan's first North Atlantic destination. His new position of responsibility as a coxswain and the new unknowns were ahead of him. He had to stow all thoughts of home and family into the dark corners of his mind. He needed his complete attention focused on his coxswain responsibilities.

The latest war news Bryan received before departing on his next convoy was that the war activities were slowing down. Two significant war events occurred while Bryan was en route during UGS-7's voyage home. The Axis forces in North Africa had surrendered and the small island outpost of Malta was reclaimed by the Allies. The Mediterranean was thereby reopened to Allied shipping. The Germans also pulled their U-boats out of the Battle of the Atlantic on May 23, 1943. The Mediterranean was now considered safe for the massive shipments needed in support of the European offensive. For five thousand years, the Mediterranean had been the arena of great sea battles, and, in World War II, that historic reputation did not change. The tide had finally shifted in favor of the Allies. Bryan was hopeful that this would be his final convoy voyage and that it would not have the unrelenting pressures of underwater and aerial attacks that he had previously experienced.

The departure destinations for Bryan's third convoy on the *Esso Montpelier* were the United Kingdom ports of Glasgow, Scotland, and Avonmouth and Hull in England. Coxswain Bryan did not provide written journals on this convoy but spoke later about the significance of the cold icy weather and his fear of the icebergs the convoy encountered.

Armed Guard Ensign Elwyn Middleton of the *Esso Montpelier* provided the thirty-two-day voyage details describing a different menace they would confront—icebergs—now the most significant threat to the convoy and crews. The voyage report for convoy HX-242 covered their travel time from May 31 through July 1, 1943.

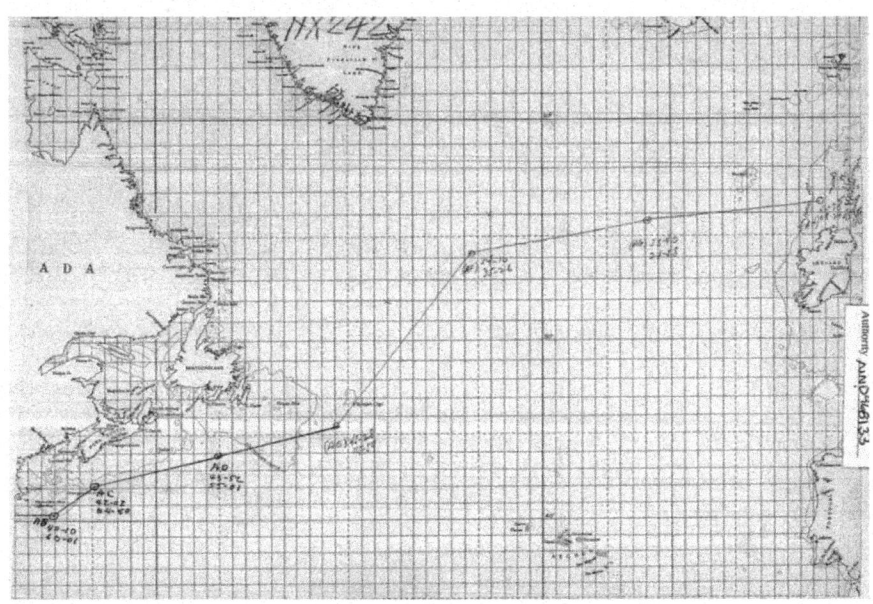

Figure 27. Map of Convoy HX-242 convoy's course from May 31 to July 1, 1943, departing from New York and arriving in the United Kingdom.

The *Esso Montpelier* departed New York harbor at 0500 hours on May 31, 1943. Once again, the vessel of 7,698 tons transported a cargo of 75,000 barrels of naval fuel oil. Convoy HX-242 included fifty-six ships, escorted by one British destroyer and four British corvettes. (Appendix VI provides the ship names and destinations of the convoy HX-242 fleet list.)

The *Esso Montpelier* took a much different route than its previous two convoys and encountered dramatically different weather. The convoy traveled north past Halifax, Nova Scotia, and Newfoundland, then turned east towards England and Scotland.

The ships ran into very heavy fog at the beginning of the voyage. On June 5 at 2045 hours, a radio message from the commodore announced that the *Nicaina* and *John A Brown*, both tankers, had hit icebergs. The *Nicaina* reported that the forward hold had twenty feet of water and they needed assistance. The *Nicaina* left the convoy and was directed to St John's, Newfoundland. The other ship, *John A. Brown,* was not severely damaged and was able to carry on with the voyage. Rough seas, icy-cold weather conditions, fog, and icebergs continued to plague convoy HX-242. The ship's crew was well aware that a "man overboard" signal under these conditions allowed for little chance of rescue. They passed icebergs all night. Numerous icebergs were reported ahead by the escort ships, and the convoy's speed was reduced. The slower pace was tedious and, of course, delayed arrival. However, for the remainder of the trip, the ships were able to avoid the icebergs.

On June 14, at 1730 hours, the Irish coast came into sight. The convoy proceeded through the North Channel to the Firth of Clyde. The Firth of Clyde encloses the broadest and deepest coastal waters in the British Isles, sheltered from the Atlantic Ocean. During World War II, Glasgow and Clyde in Scotland were Britain's main entry points for Allied merchant shipping, for military personnel and equipment, and for the assembly, dispatch, and control of ocean convoys.

Sixteen days after leaving New York, the *Esso Montpelier* proceeded up the Clyde River and reached its cargo destination at 1200 hours on June 15 at the Old Kilpatrick Dock. The crew immediately began discharging cargo.

On the following day at 1840 hours, the *Esso Montpelier* departed from Gourock, the Clyde River, and Scotland with a convoy of fifty-six ships escorted by several British destroyers and corvettes. The convoy proceeded unmolested to its port of destination and arrived in New York harbor on July 1, 1943. Again, Ensign Middleton gave a positive report on the ship's crew: "Relations with the Merchant personnel were pleasant as they have been in the past. The enlisted Naval personnel performed their duties in a military and satisfactory manner, and their morale was high at all times."

For Coxswain Ernest Bryan, the crossing of the North Atlantic, although free of aerial attacks and underwater torpedo threats, had still been a worrisome voyage with the new hazard of hidden icebergs. The successful delivery of their fuel oil in Scotland, without mishap, was a hugely positive outcome for him and the crew, given the losses during their last two convoys. The sudden sinking of the *Sidi-Bel-Abbes* and the resulting loss of lives were still fresh in Bryan's mind. Witnessing the explosions and sinking next to his ship had been extremely traumatic, and it was a very close call for the *Esso Montpelier*. Bryan would never know just how close his ship had come to being *U-565*'s next target that fateful morning. In all, six ships in his previous convoys, UGS-4 and UGS-7, had not been lucky enough to escape the U-boat. Their cargos were at the bottom of the ocean. Fortunately, the *Esso Montpelier* had successfully delivered thousands of barrels of Esso aviation gasoline and their cargo to both Oran and Algiers, threading their way through treacherous waters.

Once the *Esso Montpelier* safely docked in New York harbor, Coxswain Bryan had acquired thirty-two more days at sea and was awaiting new orders. He knew the oil tanker had been ordered to return to the United Kingdom ports; however, Ensign Middleton, Bryan, and several of the other men had been detached from the ship, and new replacements had been assigned to the *Esso Montpelier* for their next convoy voyage. In all, the transportation record of the *Esso Montpelier* shows that it completed sixty-two voyages from 1940 to 1945.[65]

The crossing of the vast Atlantic Ocean during World War II's Battle of the Atlantic, under constant threats from the air and underwater, was no doubt an ongoing mental ordeal for all ships' crew members. The dark depths of the Atlantic Ocean were the burial grounds for many ships and their crew. Vera's worry over her dream, which occurred at the exact time of Bryan's experience with KptLt. Franken and the *U-565*, was a story retold many times later to family and friends. In later years, Bryan's crewmate William Hollenback was surprised on hearing this story about the abruptly canceled torpedo attack by *U-565*. "I've never forgotten the explosion and sinking of that ship next to us. We lost too many men that day," he stated. "We never knew when our time was going to be up, but, thankfully, that was not our time."

Hollenback recollected that he had completed eight convoys in total by the end of the war. Besides the Mediterranean route and the Atlantic route, he also traveled the Pacific Ocean, the Indian Ocean, and the Arctic. He referred to the Arctic convoys as the "suicide missions" since only 50 percent of the Armed Guard returned. "Twenty-five-foot waves out there!" Hollenback said, remembering those horrific times. "Had to chip ice off the guns, day and night, during the Murmansk run. We needed to unload our cargo in Russia. And we did."[66]

Too many sailors gave their lives in their efforts to transport critically needed cargo to the Allied forces during World War II. The death toll on these silent heroes was at its highest at the end of 1943.

The US Navy Armed Guard and Merchant Marine crews paid a heavy price in reaching their objectives. If the U-boats had prevailed, the Allies could not have been successful in the war against Germany. Winston

Churchill notably summarized the German U-boats' role and the Battle of the Atlantic: "The only thing that ever really frightened me during the war was the U-boat peril."[67]

CHAPTER TWELVE

The Defeat of the U-Boat

"I take luck as a precious gift, without becoming overbearing or reckless, and if it ever leaves me, it does not mean that everything is lost. Then I can prove that I am as brave as my brothers."

-Wilhelm Franken, March 1943

T he day after *U-565* sank two ships during their eighth patrol, FdU sent the following message: "To Franken: Bravo!" *U-565*'s crew briefly celebrated but then continued their patrol.

Several more convoy alerts, identifying potential targets, were received. However, for ten days, aircraft detection and daily crash dives continued as the submarine made its way to find new targets. Finally, on May 1, *U-565* had its first chance to attack a tanker convoy. Franken fired several torpedoes but achieved only a "possible hit" due to the long distance to the targets. Once again, for another six days, aircraft continued to plague them, looming overhead and keeping *U-565* submerged. On May 5, Franken reported that their supply of potash cartridges had shrunk dramatically. (Potash cartridges are used to decrease critical levels of carbon dioxide in submarines through the use of their ventilation fans.) He attempted to keep the U-boat submerged without having to surface to renew the air. Franken reported, "The strain on the crew is such that I cannot repeat the experiment in the future."

Finally, on May 8, another small convoy presented itself. However, due to aircraft overhead, *U-565* was forced to act quickly and made a three-fan shot on a freighter. Franken discharged all three torpedoes from torpedo Tubes I, II, and IV in a "fan" pattern (versus several consecutive shots) in an attempt to make at least one hit, followed by an immediate crash dive. The hasty attempt failed.[68]

Franken relayed the following radio messages to FdU:

May 9, 0352 hours. Three-miss on freighter. Have begun return transit. -Franken-

On May 11, 1711 hours. To FdU: One man - advanced appendicitis. Highest speed. Point Caesar as early as 0430 hours.

0109 hours – Condition serious.

0145 hours Point Caesar. Running in. Request barrier open and Doctor.

0127 hours–Avoidance maneuver for unknown vessel headed for Spezia on changing courses.

Radio Message from FdU:

Franken: Barrier is open from 0230 hours and marked with red and green. Vorposten Boot [coastal patrol boat] with Doctor runs to meet you.

0350 hours – Passed outer barrier Spezia.

0400 hours—Disembarked with the patient.

On May 12, 1943, KptLt. Franken and the crew of *U-565* returned to La Spezia from their eighth patrol. They had been at sea when the award of the Knight's Cross was delivered by a radio message. News of their success preceded their return home. Celebrations began for their sinking of the two convoy ships: the American freighter *Michigan* and the Free French troop vessel *Sidi-Bel-Abbes*. *U-565*'s previous patrols' successes included the sinking of the British tanker *Seminole*, as well as the American Liberty freighter *Nathanael Greene*. Franken shared credit with the Luftwaffe for their assistance in destroying the *Nathanael Greene* with an aerial torpedo. In total, Franken and *U-565* had the destruction of 30,450 tons of Allied ships and cargo to their credit. He had become a hero on April 20, 1943, with two sinkings—something Hitler could add to his fifty-fourth birthday celebration.

Reports from the FdU Italien (Italy) on the KTB (Franken's combat reports) provided high praise for Franken for an "excellently executed patrol, which placed very high demands on the Kommandant and crew."

The use of the torpedo armament was also praised. "The operation on the convoy April 19/20 deserves special recognition. The decision of the Kommandant to initially give up the attack in the bright full moon night and maneuver ahead for submerged day attack despite hostile locating in the sharply monitored sea area was bold; the unwavering will to succeed, excellent tactical understanding, confidence in himself and the crew, were decisive for the success. The attack brought on the next morning by the screen at close range to the valuable targets was carried out excellently," reported Konteradmiral (Rear Admiral) Leo Kreisch. (Appendix VII provides the translation of the original commendation for Franken.) Kreisch held the position Leader of U-Boats, Mediterranean, for FdU Italien (February 1942 to January 1944), which was operationally subordinate to the Commander of the German Naval Command, Italy.[69]

The *U-565* crew was not due to return for their ninth patrol until June 17. Until then, Franken spent time with his crew celebrating their triumphant victory. Against high odds, *U-565* had come out of their last Mediterranean patrol intact. Few other experiences can bring men closer together than staring death in the face and surviving. The crew held their U-boat commander in high esteem.

These victories earned Franken the Knight's Cross of the Iron Cross for his "remarkable services in troop leadership." Less than 10 percent of U-boat commanders received the prestigious medal. KptLt. Wilhelm Franken had realized his childhood dreams; he had become a hero like those in the myths and legends he had loved as a youth in the Teutoburg Forest.

In addition to his military recognition and award, Franken was also featured in a local newspaper.

VERLEIHUNG DES RITTERKREUZES – EIN STOLZER TAG!

FÜR KOMMANDANT UND BESATZUNG

Kapitänleutnant Franken

Der mit dem Ritterkreuz ausgezeichnete U-Bootkommandant aus Brackwede

Wieder wurde, wie wir schon mitteilten, ein Sohn unserer Heimat, und zwar Kapitänleutnant Wilhelm Franken mit dem Ritterkreuz des Eisernen Kreuzes ausgezeichnet. Der 28jährige U-Boot-Kommandant erzielte durch den beispielhaften Schneid und gaben Angriffsgeist, mit der er alle seine Unternehmungen durchführte, hervorragende Erfolge. Sein U-Boot versenkte bisher einen Truppentransporter, einen Tanker, vier Frachter und zwei Segler mit insgesamt 45 000 BRT. sowie einen britischen Zerstörer. Außerdem wurden zwei Frachter mit zusammen 20 000 BRT. torpediert, deren Sinken sehr wahrscheinlich ist. Ferner hat Kapitänleutnant Franken ein mehrmotoriges Kampfflugzeug abgeschossen und ein weiteres beschädigt.

Der junge U-Bootkommandant, von dessen Heldentaten die Heimat mit Gefühlen des Stolzes und der Dankbarkeit vernahm, wurde in B.-Schildesche am 11. September 1914 geboren, während sein Vater, der den Weltkrieg an der Front von 1914–1918 als Offizier mitmachte, im Felde stand. Später wurde der Vater, Rektor August Franken, Leiter der Mittelschule in Brackwede, die Wilhelm Franken bis zu seinem Uebertritt in die Helmholtz-Oberrealschule in Bielefeld besuchte. Nach dem Abitur und nachdem er das Latinum bestanden, widmete er sich in Kiel dem Studium der Medizin, empfing hier die Anregung, Marineoffizier zu werden und verwirklichte damit einen Berufswunsch, der ihn schon immer vorgeschwebt hatte. Er erhielt seine Ausbildung in Mürwick und trat eine Weltreise an. Vor Kriegsausbruch schon war er zum Leutnant z. S. befördert worden. Im April 1942 erfolgte die Beförderung des bewährten und mit dem EK I und II ausgezeichneten Offiziers zum U-Bootkommandanten. Schon bei der ersten Feindfahrt fielen ihm zwei Frachter zur Beute. Seine hervorragenden Leistungen im Dienst der U-Bootwaffe haben nun die verdiente Anerkennung durch die Verleihung des Ritterkreuzes gefunden. Kapitänleutnant Franken, den viele familiäre und freundschaftliche Bande an die Heimat fesseln, ist seit dem Sommer 1942 mit einer Pfarrerstochter aus Bremen verheiratet.

Foto: Worbonn.

Figure 28. Newspaper article in honor of KptLt. Wilhelm
Franken, recipient of the Knight's Cross.

The article is translated as follows:

Awarding of the Knight's Cross - A proud day!
For Commander and Crew

Kapitänleutnant Franken

The submarine commander from Brackwede who was awarded the Knight's Cross.

Again, as we announced, a son of our home, namely Kapitänleutnant Wilhelm Franken, was awarded the Knight's Cross of the Iron Cross. The 28-year-old submarine commander achieved day-to-day success thanks to the exemplary courage and tough attack spirit with which he maintained on all his patrols. His submarine has so far sunk a troop carrier, a tanker, four freighters, and two sailing vessels with a total of 45,000 tons, as well as a British destroyer. Also, two freighters with a total of 20,000 tons were torpedoed, which were likely to sink. Furthermore, a multi-engine fighter plane was shot down by Kapitänleutnant Franken and another damaged...

Before the outbreak of war, he was promoted to Leutnant zur See [lieutenant junior grade]. In April 1942, the proven officer, who was awarded the Iron Cross I and II Class, was promoted to submarine commander. Already on the first war patrol, two freighters fell prey to him. His outstanding achievements in the service of the submarine weapon have now received the recognition he deserved by being awarded the Knight's Cross. Kapitänleutnant Franken, whom many familiar and friendly ties bind to home, has been married to a pastor's daughter from Bremen since the summer of 1942.

With over one hundred U-boats at sea, Allied losses in the Atlantic for March 1943 alone reached the alarming figure of 627,000 gross tons, nearly 20 percent of the losses for the entire year. However, success for the U-boats was quickly coming to an end. The Allies finally defeated Axis forces in Tunisia in mid-May 1943, thereby gaining control of all of North Africa. Subsequently, the Mediterranean U-boats achieved very little success. In March, twelve Allied vessels had been sunk by U-boats in the Mediterranean, totaling 46,800 tons. The tonnage lost by the Allies in April decreased dramatically with the highest tonnage score from Franken and *U-565*.[70] Franken sank

10,000 tons of Allied ships and cargo during *U-565*'s eighth patrol. Although the number of operational U-boats peaked in May at 240, of which 118 were at sea, their ability to sink Allied ships continued to decline.[71]

Then, in an incredible turn of events, forty-one U-boats were sunk or destroyed in May 1943.[72] Admiral Karl Dönitz, now five months as commander in chief of the German Navy, recognized the defeat. It was clear that the Allied air strength in the Atlantic, consisting of new long-range planes and carrier-borne aircraft, had increased enormously. The long-range aircraft could spot U-boats, using specially developed radar, and could direct convoy escort ships to attack the U-boats, or they could attack the U-boats themselves.[73] The combined growth in numbers of Allied ships, airpower, and technological developments in anti-submarine warfare dramatically improved convoy protection. And timely information regarding enemy activity provided by ULTRA supported the Allies in turning the tide against the U-boats. On May 24, 1943, known as "Black May," Dönitz ordered a temporary halt to U-boat operations in the Atlantic to recoup, stating, "Our losses… have reached an intolerable level." Overall, between April and July 1943, 109 of the 240 operational U-boats were lost.

The U-boats were never able to regain their former strength. Effectively, this series of events put an end to the widely spread U-boat attacks in the Battle of the Atlantic. U-boat operations in the Mediterranean effectively ended in 1943. Even so, Hitler insisted that the Mediterranean "continue to be maintained" with twenty-plus U-boats in operation. It is believed that Hitler wanted to protect the coastline to preserve U-boat training areas,

Figure 29. KptLt. Wilhelm Franken, upon departing his *U-565* command and relocating to Kiel as a staff officer within the BdU U-boat command in October 1943.

given his belief in Dönitz's ability to turn the tide of war with the production of a newer type of submarine. The minimal strength of U-boat operations was not the end of the threat in the Atlantic, but the danger of U-boat attack was greatly diminished.

U-565 was one of a select number of U-boats still required to continue patrolling in the Mediterranean. KptLt. Franken and his crew's ninth patrol left the base in La Spezia two days before his first wedding anniversary. The patrol lasted thirty-seven days, from June 17 to July 23, with a new return destination of Toulon, France.

Besides La Spezia and Salamis, Toulon and Pula, Croatia, were also serving as major German submarine bases. On August 1, 1943, the 29th Flotilla fully shifted its headquarters from La Spezia to Toulon, where it used the former French Navy base for patrols in the western Mediterranean. KptLt. Franken's tenth patrol, which lasted twenty-five days, departed out of Toulon on September 7, 1943. *U-565* did not sink any additional Allied ships during their last two patrols. Franken's career as a veteran U-boat commander would soon be coming to an end. His crew knew that their exceptional commander was being promoted and transferred to BdU headquarters and a staff position. While completing his final mission and while *U-565* was on its passage home, Franken wrote in his journals on September 27, 1943:

> On-Board 27.9.43—It is going to be a while until I mail this letter since I started writing it at sea. However, we are already heading towards the harbor, so it will all be over in a couple of days. After a couple of days full of concentration and tension, we are finally calming down. My diary is almost finished. Since the captain is not required anymore after the ship reaches the harbor, I can start writing letters. Although this is the first time I started writing while at sea. I do not know if it is right since you should always focus on what is ahead of you and if the crew would find out about it, they would probably call me a saboteur.

I am still underwater. The sound of war, the air and sea bombs, the engines of a destroyer, the annoying noise of sonars and radars, everything took longer than expected. We are slowly gaining distance. The crew can finally start washing their clothes since they all need to be clean when we arrive in the harbor. It gets really bad when the smell gets combined with the right amount of "4711 or juchten" [animal leather and cologne]. Not even the most stinging southern mosquitoes dare to venture out.

Today is a very memorable one for me. It has been two years since our boat has passed Gibraltar. Many things have changed since then, but one thing is staying the same: The will to make the best out of every situation no matter how bad it is. Now I hear them calling that the food is ready, Leipzig Allerlei [German vegetable dish]. Since the meals onboard are sacred and the appetite of the captain has a significant impact on the morale of the crew, you will understand that I am going to end here now.

-Franken[74]

CHAPTER THIRTEEN

The Tragic Loss of a Hero

"What lies behind him and what lies before him are tiny, compared to what lies within him."

–Ralph Waldo Emerson

In October 1943, Franken left command of *U-565* to become a staff officer of the Befehlshaber der Unterseeboote (BdU) Submarine Command in Kiel. Leaving his crew was not easy, as there was a tremendous camaraderie between Franken and the men. A letter written by one of his crew expressed their admiration and respect:

> Through ten patrols against the enemy as our commanding officer on U-565, you set for us a shining example of fear of God, humaneness, camaraderie, justice, courage, and strength of character. All men on board gave you their full confidence. We were absolutely convinced of your leadership abilities. Your keen mind, your courage, and the strength of your soul allowed us to survive even when our boat seemed almost lost.[75]

Franken left his men with a heavy heart and a promise to stay connected in the future—a commitment he would not forget.

With his U-boat patrols behind him, Franken would now operate within the U-boat arm at U-boat Headquarters, reporting for duty in the Training Command under Admiral Hans-Georg von Friedeburg. Fortunately, the timing of the move to Kiel allowed for closer contact with his wife and family. His wife, Waltraut, was now four months pregnant. Once he began in his new position, Franken added to his war journal—now from the perspective of a U-boat command staff officer. While temporarily reporting for duty at the command post in Athens, Greece, the last German-occupied area until October 1944, Franken wrote in his journal:

Athens Nov 10, 1943— From the Wehrmacht report [High Command mass-media communiqué], it can already be seen that…something is going on. That is why there has been more to do than usual in the last few days. At least you always have to be present at the command post. This also includes sleeping there. I much rather prefer sleeping in the hotel, because after the submarine, I crave a good night of sleep.

Yesterday I had a very nice experience, which threw a ray of light into the war despite the sorrows of the situation. I had to interrogate three captured Englishmen of a sunken English destroyer. They might have been amazed when I knew more about their vehicle than they did. Above all, I was able to tell them about small events and encounters with submarines; I often met their destroyer on the route Alexandria-Tobruk and last but not least, most recently in Salerno. After a while, the interrogation turned into a very comfortable conversation over common war experiences of survivors and victims of war, Kriegerverein [Warriors' Association]. They rejoiced that they had survived from it all and I did the same, for their destroyer had more often covered me with depth charges![76]

Franken kept his promise to the men of *U-565* and also traveled to Salamis in November 1943. He greeted his former crew members after they returned from their first patrol under their new commander. The men sincerely appreciated his continued leadership and always spoke highly of him.

KptLt. Franken's leadership and compassion continued to manifest themselves in other instances, as an example when he spoke up for a fellow U-boat commander. The *U-154* commander was under attack for a crime of sedition and cowardice, triggering formal legal proceedings and arrest on January 20, 1944. Franken, along with a few other officers, came to Oskar-Heinz Kusch's defense when the U-boat high command refused to intervene.

The officers and many others in U-boat service resented the fact that neither Dönitz nor Admiral von Friedeburg nor Rear Admiral Godt did anything to help Kusch during the court-martial. None of the U-boat commanding officers chose to see him or to hear his side of the story.[77] KptLt. Franken, serving on Admiral von Friedeburg's staff, was quite critical of the accuser, Kusch's U-boat Lieutenant, Ulrich Abel. Abel's report described suspicious incidents during a patrol including criticism of Germany's leadership. Franken was tasked to provide an expert opinion on Kusch's "lack of aggressive spirit" charge. After reviewing U-154's war diaries and with little time to examine Kusch's military actions in question, Franken found the evidence inconclusive. His findings described "moments of some inexperience and indecisiveness" on Kusch's part, but no indication of "personal cowardice." Franken's professional assessment forced the charge of "lack of aggressive spirit" to be dismissed during the court-martial. The allegations of sedition remained. Kusch was accused of "continuously and publicly paralyzing or eroding the will of the German people to self-assert themselves militarily and undermining the discipline of the Germany Military."[78]

The court found Oskar-Heinz Kusch guilty and, on January 26, 1944, ruled his execution instead of prison time. Kusch was sentenced to death, and, on May 12, 1944, a firing squad carried out the sentence in Kiel-Holtenau.[79] The news about Kusch was devastating to many in the U-boat service. It did not settle well with many officers who felt this was an unjust fate and could have been rectified. The verdict was especially distressing and burdensome for a compassionate leader of men such as Wilhelm Franken.

With the war still raging, Franken plunged into his new duties. The excitement of the birth of his daughter on February 11, 1944, added to Franken and Waltraut's joy and responsibilities. Fortunately, support from both their families kept his wife and daughter safe while he attended to his duties in Kiel headquarters. In July, their happiness doubled when Waltraut became pregnant again with their second child. Despite the troubled political times, Franken worked hard to keep his family safe and separate from his headquarters staff responsibilities.

On July 20, 1944, the assassination attempt on Hitler's life highlighted the broader effort to overthrow his regime. The code name Operation Valkyrie referred to a part of the German conspiracy whose purpose was to seize control of the government and seek more favorable peace terms from the Allies. Hitler's death, as opposed to his arrest, was required to free German soldiers from their loyalty oath. When the plot failed, the civilian and military officials involved were captured and executed seven months later. Germany's internal politics were clearly in disarray, as Allied forces continued to push forward in the war.

Franken's new staff position allowed him to stay abreast of the dire circumstances affecting his former crewmates. They were no longer the hunters but the hunted. U-boat operations were severely limited, not only because of Allied anti-submarine hunter-killer groups (additional convoy support groups of warships with an escort carrier in each) actively deployed and more British aircraft sweeping the seas but also by shortages of fuel and trained crewmen. And the loss of French ports for safe harbor and the destruction of U-boat pens (bases that acted as bunkers to protect U-boats from air attack) by Allied aircrafts' bombing efforts added to U-boat losses. After the invasion of southern France on August 15, 1944, the United States Army Air Forces (USAAF) and Allied air raids eliminated the eleven U-boats remaining in the Mediterranean. The final three U-boats to be destroyed included *U-565* based in Salamis in September 1944.[80] *U-565* had one of the longest unbroken careers of any U-boat in the Mediterranean, serving in this theatre from November 1941 until September 1944. Unlike many other U-boats that had lost men due to accidents and various other causes, *U-565* did not suffer any casualties until its last battle.[81]

The end of *U-565* came almost a year after Franken had left his command. The U-boat was scuttled with three depth charges in the Skaramagas

Bay, Greece, on September 30, 1944, after being severely damaged by bombs from two US air raids on Salamis on September 19 and 24, 1944. Five crew members were killed, and the number of survivors was unknown. The remaining men were forced to retreat and embarked on an arduous journey home through Yugoslavia, where seven men died fighting on foot against partisans. The others arrived safely at their home garrisons of Neustadt/ Holstein and Plön, Germany, in December 1944. Once again, Franken kept his word and traveled to their locations to show sympathy and support. He shook hands with each man, offered words of appreciation and comfort, and wished all a relaxing holiday at home with loved ones.[82]

On January 1, 1945, after spending the holidays with his wife and family, KptLt. Franken received a promotion from Kapitänleutnant (Captain Lieutenant) to Korvettenkapitän (Lieutenant Commander), the lowest rank of senior officers. His new rank and responsibilities at German Submarine Command Kiel were the result of his excellent previous service.

Shockingly, a mere twelve days after his promotion, Franken died while onboard a barracks ship, the *Daressalem,* docked in Kiel harbor where he was billeted as his living quarters.

On January 13, 1945, a fire broke out on the ship. The fire took Franken's life, as well as the lives of two other U-boat commanders and BdU staff members: OLt. Georg von Bitter and Knight's Cross winner KptLt. Siegfried Lüdden.

The tragic incident was later described by one of Franken's U-565 crewmembers, Helmut Jacksch:

> The unlucky ship was initially a cargo ship carrying passengers. The 'disaster' room where our commander was killed was a large semicircular entertainment room for passengers. A film was to be shown on the night of the disaster. However, an air-raid alarm forced the evacuation of the ship and the entertainment room.

After the warning, the film was to be screened. There occurred an explosion in a closed space. With the sudden gust of flame and the immediate removal of oxygen from the air, some personnel in the entertainment room were no longer able to evacuate. Possibly this was due to the intense smoke and lack of oxygen.[83]

It is believed the fire was caused by the movie projector film. The cellulose nitrate film, which burns quickly with a hot intense flame and particularly toxic smoke, created large quantities of poisonous gases. An attempt by one of the men to smash the porthole window glass failed. Franken was not supposed to have been there that tragic night, according to a report reviewed by one of Franken's *U-565* crewmembers. He had temporarily taken over duty for another officer that evening. He was, therefore, in the room at the time of the accident. The only men able to escape the room in time were those closest to the exit doors.[84]

Wilhelm Franken's ill-fated end was devastating for his young family and his parents and siblings. Sadly, his daughter was only one month shy of her first birthday, and Waltraut was pregnant with their second child.

Franken's successful U-boat career in the Mediterranean included a total of ten patrols and 269 days at sea. He and his loyal crew of *U-565* sank four Allied ships (12,887 tons) and damaged two other ships (17,565 tons). The men of *U-565* would never forget the honorable leadership of KrvKpt. Wilhelm Franken and strove to keep his memory alive. A radio operator from *U-565* whose name is unknown wrote the following letter, telling of his love and respect for Franken and his family:[85]

In Memoriam Wilhelm Franken—Every life bears in it the seed of the next life and our souls depart to allow for a new one to take its place for all eternity.

More than four decades have passed, yet the experiences that connected me to you remain distinct in my memory. During those ten patrols you exhausted your physical and mental strength so that a change of command became necessary. We knew that you took leave of us with a heavy heart. We had mixed feelings when you left. Your promise to keep in touch with us in the future comforted us, and you kept your word. All the way until your premature death, you remained deeply connected to us. When we returned to Salamis in November 1943 from our first patrol under your successor as commanding officer, you were there to welcome us at the pier to our distinct surprise and delight. After all, we had imagined you to be by then a thousand miles away back home.

When we returned from our leave, you were no longer among us. The news hit us like a blow out of the blue. A sad fate had wrenched you from a life full of hope and promise. We felt as if paralyzed. Pain and deep sorrow filled our hearts. We had lost a cherished friend and comrade. Yes, you were gone, but we men of your boat have honored you and your memory to this day.

In the course of our patrols, of all the men on board, I was always closest to you, because as the most junior radioman and according to ancient tradition, I took care of your cabin and looked after your personal needs aboard and ashore. When in quiet moments at sea your thoughts strayed to the situation at home, I was the one to sense it first. You would then ask me to play a record on our loudspeaker system that only you could hear in your cabin. You once told me that your wife had actually sung that song for you. In those moments, much too rare, you gained new energy to meet your responsibilities. Your wife, like you, came from a profoundly Christian family. Her father served as a pastor in Bremen. Daily prayers governed your life and made you strong. We men felt this strength, and it gave us a sense of security.

On several occasions during the war, I had occasion to meet your relatives, including your wife and your parents. I was always warmly received and rewarded with expressions of concern and affection. These visits extended well into the postwar period.

Figure 30. Wilhelm Franken's Gravestone 11.9.1914 – 13.01.1945, Kiel War Cemetery, Kiel, Block VII Grab 366.

Figure 31. The Kiel War Cemetery in which Franken was buried in Kiel-Nordfriedhof, Germany, where 3,000 German casualties from both world wars also lie. A veterans' memorial at the cemetery is dedicated to the 30,000 Kriegsmarine men who died for their country.

In those days I lived in Herford not far from Bremen. I remember well how my visits always brought out a sense of genuine welcome filling the room and especially the times when your mother would demonstrate how to use a traditional wooden spinning wheel with her well-practiced fingers. It was always a delight visiting your mother even after your father had died. You were always a topic of our conversations. I adored your mother as she always spread such kindness and a sense of humanity.

I also visited with your wife in those first years after the war. She was then living with your parents in a beautiful old parsonage in Bremen. There I met your daughter Andrea, born on November 1, 1944, who had to grow up without ever knowing her father.

One day your brother Ernst got in touch with me. We first corresponded with each other and then met at his home in Hamburg. On those occasions I learned what family traditions and family togetherness really mean. Those who have left us continue to live in our hearts.[86]

CHAPTER FOURTEEN

War Comes to an End

"The Battle of the Atlantic was the dominating factor all through the war. Never for one moment could we forget that everything happening elsewhere, on land, at sea, in the air, depended ultimately on its outcome."

-Winston S. Churchill, *Closing the Ring*

The Battle of the Atlantic's beginning of the end was underway a year before Franken's death in January 1945. The years of 1944 and 1945 held many setbacks for the Axis powers as a result of the first high-level Allied conference that planned for the war's end.

On November 30, 1943, President Roosevelt attended the Allied Nations Conference, held in the Soviet Union's embassy in Tehran, Iran. He met with Prime Minister Winston Churchill and Soviet Premier Joseph Stalin. It was the first of the World War II conferences of the "Big Three" Allied leaders (the United States, the United Kingdom, and the Soviet Union). Agreements on how to win the war were proposed, and decisions were made to move forward. During the Tehran Conference (codenamed Eureka),[87] Roosevelt also presented one of his visions for the future. He outlined for Churchill and Stalin his plan for a proposed organization comprising a union of nations. The organization would be dominated by "four policemen" (the United States, the United Kingdom, China, and the Soviet Union) who "would have the power to deal immediately with any threat to the peace and any sudden emergency which requires action."[88] In support, the Soviet Union committed to joining the war against Japan and expressed support for Roosevelt's plans. This conference served as one of the first conversations surrounding the formation of what would become the United Nations.

The Allied Nations Conference meeting ended on December 1, 1943. President Roosevelt departed Iran on December 8, 1943, for Sicily, landing at the Castelvetrano Airfield to meet with his generals.

Figure 32. President Franklin Roosevelt, speaking with General Dwight Eisenhower during the president's visit to the 314 Troop Carrier Group, Mediterranean Theater of Operations (MTO), at Castelvetrano, Sicily, on December 8, 1943.

The most significant outcome of the Allied conference was the agreement on the opening of the second front against Nazi Germany by invading northern France. The battle plan commenced on June 6, 1944, and the battle codenamed Operation Overlord—also known as D-Day—began. Allied General Dwight Eisenhower commanded the largest invasion force in history. More than 160,000 Allied soldiers (American, British, Canadian, and others) landed on the beaches of Normandy, France, to begin the operation that would ultimately liberate Western Europe from Nazi Germany's control. The deadly struggle dragged on for another eleven months, ending in May 1945, once all of northern France was liberated. The Normandy landings have been called the beginning of the end of the war in Europe.

During the liberation of Western Europe, Hitler launched a surprise attack against the Americans on the Western Front in Belgium on December 16, 1944. Known as The Battle of the Bulge, the devastation in lives lost lasted six weeks, ending on January 28, 1945, and was called "the greatest American battle of the war" by Winston Churchill. This battle was Hitler's last major offensive of World War II. Both the Allies and the Germans suffered enormous casualties. According to the United States Department of Defense, more than one million Allied troops, including some 500,000 Americans, fought in the Battle of the Bulge. Approximately 19,000 Allied soldiers were killed in action, 47,500 wounded, and 23,000 were missing. About 100,000 Germans were killed, wounded, or captured. Hitler failed in his aim to divide Britain, France, and the United States in their push toward Germany and thus paved the way to victory for the Allies. At that time, few people other than Hitler believed that Germany could still win the war.[89]

Figure 33. President Franklin D. Roosevelt is shown in the front of the jeep, talking to General Henry H. "Hap" Arnold, Chief of the Army Air Forces, during the president's visit to the 314 Troop Carrier Group at Castelvetrano, Sicily, in December 1943. Behind them on the right is General Dwight D. Eisenhower, sitting in the rear seat of the jeep. Generals George S. Patton and Mark W. Clark are in the background.

As the Allies pushed toward Berlin, President Franklin Roosevelt died of a cerebral hemorrhage at age sixty-three. Unfortunately, he would not realize his final goal of an Allied victory. On April 12, 1945, Harry S. Truman took office and became the thirty-third president of the United States. Less than a month later, the defeat of Nazi Germany came on May 7, and victory in Europe (V-E Day) was declared on May 8, 1945.

Days before Germany's surrender, there were approximately 375 U-boats still operational on the morning of May 4, 1945, when Dönitz sent the order, "Stop all hostile action against Allied shipping." When the order for the cease-fire was given, only sixty-four U-boats were at sea, of which fifty-six subsequently surrendered in Allied or neutral ports. Dönitz sent a surrender signal to his U-boat commanders, "You have fought like lions." To his U-boat crewmen, he wrote, "Undefeated and spotless you lay down your arms after a heroic battle without equal.... Comrades! Preserve your U-boat spirit, with which you have fought courageously, stubbornly, and imperturbably through the years for the good of the Fatherland. Long live Germany!"[90]

Some U-boats that did not get the word continued to torpedo Allied ships until May 7, by which time twelve of them had been sunk. Of those last U-boats, a total of 156 surrendered, and 219 were scuttled by their crew. Allied air bombardment and mines destroyed the other U-boats, and, according to some reports, three U-boats escaped to Argentina.[91]

Following Germany's surrender on May 7 and the declaration of victory in Europe, a series of telegrams arrived from Winston Churchill for President Truman. Extracts from the telegrams follow, recognizing the agony of the long struggles in the Battle of the Atlantic and commending the success of the united Allies' heroic efforts in support of Great Britain.

[Telegram extracts]

With the surrender of Germany, the Battle of the Atlantic has ended. German U-boats have ceased to operate and are now proceeding under Allied Orders. Beginning in September 1939, it has been a long relentless struggle. A struggle demanding not only the utmost courage, daring, and endurance, but also the highest scientific and technical skill. Germany's object was to cut the Allied sea communications, upon which the maintenance of the Allied war effort depended. This included the movements and supply of armies and air forces during successful campaigns on four continents. Losses have been heavy both in lives and materials. At the peak in 1941 and 1942, the issue of the struggle hung in the balance. On the other hand, over 700 U-boats have been sunk, and others destroyed by the Germans in the final stage. Most of these successes were achieved by the combined Allied naval and air forces working in close co-operation, others are due to mines laid from aircraft and ships, others due to bombings in harbor, and marine dangers. But success was achieved. Thanks to the sailors and airmen, the scientists and technicians, the shipbuilders, and factory workers, the convoys reached their destination. They enabled the soldiers and the airmen to fulfill the promise made early in the war that given the tools we would finish the job. We, President and Prime Minister, in our last joint statement on the U-boat war, can now report the Allies have finished the job.[92]

With the war in Europe at an end, the United States prepared for the air, land, and sea invasion of Japan, where one million casualties were expected. After relentless bombing, Japan still would not surrender. However, President Truman decided to use the atomic bomb to end the war as quickly as possible and thus save countless American lives.

On August 6, 1945, a newly developed weapon that had been assembled by scientists was loaded by the Navy Seabees into a US Army Air Force B-29 bomber named the *Enola Gay*. A short time later, the *Enola Gay* took off with its secret load from Tinian's North Field airfield in the Mariana Islands and started on its mission to Japan. Later in the day, the mission ended with the dropping of the first atomic bomb on Hiroshima, Japan. The Soviet Union declared war on Japan three days later, and the United States dropped a second atomic bomb on Nagasaki, Japan, a key ship-manufacturing hub, on August 9, 1945. This historic event sealed the fate of Japan. World War II is recognized as having ended with the armistice on August 14, 1945, and with the formal surrender of Japan on September 2, 1945. The Japanese Instrument of Surrender was signed during a ceremony on the deck of the battleship USS *Missouri* in Tokyo Bay, Japan. World War II, the most devastating event in human history, was over.

Figure 34. The signing of the Instrument of Surrender on the battleship USS *Missouri* off the coast of Tokyo, Japan.

Winston Churchill sent a personal telegram three days later to President Truman, praising America's leadership and heroic deeds. Churchill wrote,

> I must also give expression to our British sentiments about all the valiant and magnanimous deeds of the United States of America under the leadership of President Roosevelt, so steadfastly carried forward by you Mr. President since his death in action. They will forever stir the hearts of Britain in all quarters of the world in which they dwell and will I am certain lead to

even closer affections and ties than those that have been fanned into flame by the two world wars through which we have passed with harmony and elevation of mind.[93]

The overall death count from World War II is uncertain to this day. Total casualties are now estimated to be over sixty million military personnel and civilians. Although the numbers vary from many sources, the nations suffering the highest estimated losses were: Soviet Union, forty-two million; Germany, nine million; China, four million; and Japan, three million. In comparison, approximately 405,000 US military personnel and 383,000 United Kingdom military personnel died during World War II, according to the Department of Defense (as of November 2019).

Among the estimated thirteen to sixteen million United States men and women who served in the military during World War II, there were 4,183,466 US Navy personnel (390,037 US Navy officers and 3,793,429 Navy enlisted). In comparison, the US Navy Armed Guard in World War II comprised nearly 145,000 US enlisted men and officers who served in protecting merchant ships and their vital cargoes.[94]

The number of casualties related to U-boat success was kept secret during the war. The intent was to deny the enemy any information. US newspapers carried mostly the same story each week: "Two medium-sized Allied ships sunk in the Atlantic." In reality, the average for 1942 was approximately twenty-five Allied ships sunk each week. It was not until 1943 that the convoy system to protect the merchant ships became fully operational. (Appendix VIII provides a graph of North Atlantic and mid-Atlantic convoy ship losses and damages.)

The installation of additional and newer guns on these merchant ships increased along with an increase in the number of officers and trained men and the number of US Navy escort ships.

According to the *Shipping Administration Press Release* (#2514, January 1, 1946), US Merchant Marine men serving in World War II totaled 243,000. However, the numbers vary by source and range from 215,000 to 285,000 due to the lack of centralized administrative recording during the war. The merchant ships' men who made up their civilian crews included officers, deckhands, oilers, and cooks. An average merchant ship crewed with forty-two mariners. Although casualty statistics vary, an estimated 9,521 US Merchant Marine seamen died in World War II. The men of the US Merchant Marine were civilian volunteers who nonetheless gave their lives in numbers that rivaled or exceeded any branch of the uniformed military.[95]

By the end of World War II, they had sailed on 4,220 Allied merchant ships, of which more than 1,554 ships were sunk and many more damaged.

Throughout the war, the U-boats inflicted enormous damage. However, compared to the merchant ship losses, 784 out of 1,156 U-boats built ended up resting permanently on the bottom of the ocean. In addition, over 28,000 of the 40,900 German submariners who put to sea never returned—the highest casualty rate of any armed service in the history of modern war.[96]

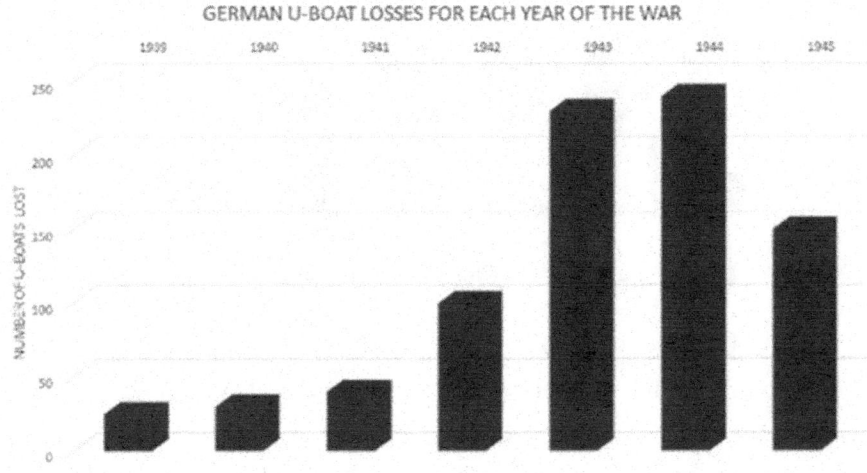

Figure 35. World War II U-boat Losses

The US Navy Armed Guard crews assigned to protect merchant ships were physically separated from their fellow US Navy seamen. They were placed in small groups aboard merchant vessels run by civilians. Due to the secrecy surrounding this "special force," the public did not understand what they did. The Navy tended to forget about them. The Armed Guard—recognized as the *unsung heroes* of the war—were continually sent into harm's way to protect and deliver the goods. An average Armed Guard crew had twenty-seven men. According to lists compiled from various sources, of the total 145,000 Armed Guard serving in World War II in defense of their country, they suffered casualties numbering 2,193 or missing in action, and 1,127 were wounded as a result of enemy action. Some sources place casualty totals even higher. The Armed Guard sustained its highest number of casualties, 1,007 men, during 1943.[97]

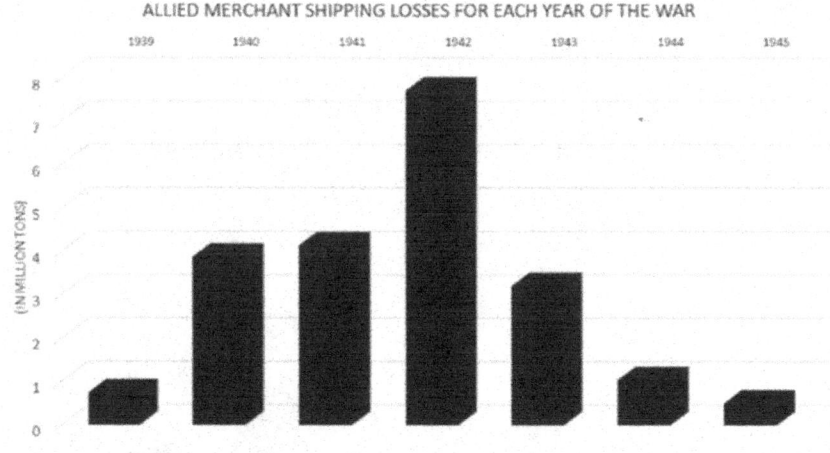

Figure 36. World War II Merchant Ship Losses

Like the Armed Guard who sailed with them, the civilian mariners of the Merchant Marine made the Allied victory in World War II possible. There were instances of friction between the Armed Guard and merchant sailors, but they were relatively rare. Together, Armed Guard crew members and merchant sailors faced the same dangers, and both knew the time might come when their survival might well depend on each other. Winston Churchill, in recognition, declared,

> …Many gallant actions and incredible feats of endurance are recorded, but the deeds of those who perished will never be known. Our merchant seamen displayed their highest qualities, and the brotherhood of the sea was never more strikingly shown than in their determination to defeat the U-boat.

EPILOGUE

Patriotism Lives On

"It is, in a way, an odd thing to honor those who died
in defense of our country, in defense of us, in wars far away.
The imagination plays a trick.
We see these soldiers in our mind as old and wise.
We see them as something like the Founding Fathers, grave
and gray-haired.

But most of them were boys when they died, and they gave
up two lives…
the one they were living and the one they would have lived.
When they died, they gave up their chance to be
husbands and fathers and grandfathers.
They gave up their chance to be revered, old men.
They gave up everything for our country, for us.
And all we can do is remember."

-Ronald Reagan, November 11, 1985

Coxswain Bryan was one of the lucky ones. He returned home from the Battle of the Atlantic along with the rest of his crewmates, but he was a changed man. Bryan remained on active duty with the US Navy Armed Guard for almost two years after returning on July 1, 1943, from his third convoy. The combined length of his foreign sea service with the Armed Guard was thirteen months, although it is unknown on which ships he served as coxswain after his promotion. Fortunately, on his return to the United States for duty, Bryan was transferred to the naval base in Jacksonville, Florida, thus allowing him to be closer to his family.

Following the end of the war, the Armed Guard, like other military units, was rapidly drawn down in size, as men were discharged from service. A few Armed Guards were kept aboard merchant vessels to maintain the guns until the weapons were removed and returned to the US Navy in 1946. Bryan's Armed Guard service ended on September 26, 1945. He then enlisted in the active US Navy Reserve. Fortunately, both of his brothers, Paul and Enoch, also returned safely from the war. Paul, who had served in the Seabees, completed his assignment and reenlisted in the US Navy on August 26, 1943, serving aboard the USS *Merak* until December 13, 1945. Enoch served in the US Army until September 12, 1945. Ultimately, all the Bryan brothers returned to Florida near their father and families.

The long absences from each other during the war had lasting effects on Ernest, Vera, and their young daughter Linda. The young couple's struggling relationship survived the hard times of war separations, and, on Bryan's return to Jacksonville, Vera became a part of his military life, going with Bryan into government housing. In October 1946, Vera gave birth to their second daughter, Sharon, while living in Hialeah, Florida.

Figure 37. Ernest (left) and his two brothers, Enoch (center) and Paul (right), enjoying a family reunion in California in 1967.

After the war, the Navy still did not recognize the Armed Guard as a full member of the US Navy family. As such, Bryan evaluated the limits of a Navy career. On November 28, 1948, he was given an honorable discharge. The following day, Bryan enlisted in the US Coast Guard in Miami, Florida. He had decided, considering his wartime service in the Armed Guard, that the Coast Guard would provide more opportunities for him in a future military career. Ultimately, this proved to be the case. Vera was now pregnant with their third child. On December 21, 1948, with his promotion to boatswain's mate 2nd class (BM2), Bryan received orders to the Coast Guard bases in San Juan, Puerto Rico, and St. Thomas, Virgin Islands. For a short time, once again, he separated from his family. Vera remained in Florida until the birth of their son, Michael, in March 1949. Shortly thereafter, Vera and the children moved to St. Thomas, once again joining Bryan in government housing. Their daughter Linda remained in Miami, living with Vera's mother to continue attending school. After a year and a half, Bryan and his family returned to Miami in December 1950, where they lived on base once again until moving to a home in Hialeah. Vera gave birth to their fourth child—another daughter, Gretchen—in June 1951. In 1953, the family moved to Pompano Beach Coast Guard Station, where Bryan served at the Hillsboro Inlet Lighthouse.

Figure 38. Senior Chief Boatswain's Mate Ernest V. Bryan, US Coast Guard, during his 1965 Coast Guard retirement ceremony at the Coast Guard Island training center in Alameda, California.

Over the years, the Coast Guard life required many more moves for Bryan and his family, not only across the United States (Texas, Louisiana, Mississippi, and California) but also to Port au Prince, Haiti. In 1958, one year after the establishment of the President Duvalier regime, Petty Officer BM1 Ernest Bryan and his family were transferred to Haiti. A "teacher at heart," Bryan helped reestablish the Haitian Coast Guard by teaching seamanship and coast-guard duties to Haitian recruits. The Haitian Coast Guard patrol boats and their crews were successfully put to use. Under Bryan's coast-guard training and leadership, they patrolled the Haitian coastline for over two years. Although the country of Haiti underwent many political and military changes through the years, the Haitian Coast Guard survived and is now established under the Haitian National Police.

The Bryan family left Haiti and moved to San Leandro, California, in 1960, for his final military reenlistment and tour of duty. Bryan retired from the Coast Guard at the Alameda Coast Guard Base as a Senior Chief Petty Officer (BMCS). He was given an honorable discharge and placed on the inactive retirement list on June 1, 1965, in Alameda, California. In total, he spent twenty-three years in active service to his county. Bryan was awarded the National Defense Medal of the United States Armed Forces for his active military time during the Korean War (June 27, 1950 to July 27, 1954) and the Vietnam Conflict (January 1, 1961 to August 14, 1974).

After his military retirement, Bryan held two civilian positions in California before fully retiring and moving to Phoenix, Arizona. His first job was as an inventory control manager with a local industrial company. The following year, he accepted a position with Loomis armored security for several years as an armed guard. Once again, Ernest Bryan was protecting valuable cargo during transportation, as he had done decades before with the US Navy Armed Guard. As a teacher to his Navy and Coast Guard recruits, his bible-study students in church, and all his children and grandchildren, Bryan helped shape and improve many lives.

Figure 39. Ernest and Vera Bryan, married sixty-six years.

Ernest and Vera's marriage lasted for sixty-six years. Always the patriot, Senior Chief Boatswain's Mate Ernest Bryan passed away with his family at his side on November 25, 2004. His military burial ceremony was conducted in the National Memorial Cemetery of Arizona, Section 60, Site 1056, in Phoenix, Arizona. Vera died four months later on March 27, 2005, and was buried at his side. Ernest and Vera's four children and their grandchildren all remained an active family unit. Their oldest daughter, Linda Dawn Dunn, passed away on December 13, 2019, after sixty-three years of marriage to her now-retired husband, Lt. Commander Jack Dunn, US Coast Guard.

This story speaks of those times in World War II when the death of the enemy was rewarded and winning was the goal. In the end, the story is not about those who failed. Instead, it is about honor—honor for those who did their duty to the best of their ability under exceptionally difficult circumstances. Win or lose, we honor those heroes who fought for their country by remembering the lessons learned and by sharing their untold stories.

Ernest Bryan never openly expressed the difficult and dangerous times he experienced during the war. Instead, he lived his life, demonstrating strong military leadership and principles, integrity, and—always—love for his country. If not for his journals and personal letters that were preserved for over seventy-five years, this story of Bryan's struggles encountered during the war and his lifelong patriotism could not be shared.

Bryan's crewmember William Hollenback shared his stories in later years and said that it was not until he was in his late fifties that the nightmares stopped haunting him. Then and only then did he begin to heal. "You cannot worry about the enemy and their personal lives. If you don't kill them, they will kill you; you just do what you were trained to do," Hollenback explained. "After the war, I had animosity towards Germany and Japan, but not now. I have had many German and Japanese friends since then. We all did what we needed to do at that time for our own countries."

Hollenback provided multiple stories of his World War II times. He was born on December 17, 1923, in Moosic, Pennsylvania, and was drafted at eighteen years of age. He completed his US Navy boot camp training in

Bainbridge, Maryland, and completed his US Navy Armed Guard gunnery training in Norfolk, Virginia. At the end of the war, Hollenback completed his four-year military enlistment and returned home. He enlisted in the US Navy Reserve after the war for ten years in an inactive status. At ninety-three years old, his pride was still evident, as he mentioned his five medals and two citations. Hollenback passed away on February 19, 2020, at the age of ninety-five.

As for Wilhelm Franken, thanks to his journals and letters shared by his U-boat crew and family, we know much about his life, leadership, compassion towards his crew, and the devastating loss felt by his family and friends upon news of his tragic death.

Most men during the war did as trained to protect lives and their country. It is important not to judge any of the people bearing different flags and how they performed under the pressures of war. The battles were fought by the men of those times, all wired together differently. Some held up better under attack than others; many lost their lives; and others carried their memories in silence, affecting their personal lives for years to come. They were all afraid. They were all human. They were all heroes.

Figure 40. Military burial site for Ernest and Vera Bryan at the National Memorial Cemetery of Arizona, Section 60, Site 1056, Phoenix, Arizona.

Appendix I

SS *Esso Montpelier* Oil Tanker

Figure 41. SS *Esso Montpelier* Oil Tanker

a) UGS-4 Convoy Fleet List

b) Armed Guard Personnel Roster

c) Guns Aboard Vessel on Departure

(a)

Fleet of 47 Merchant Vessels and 6 Escorts

Departures	Convoy	Arrivals
Hampton Roads, Jan 13, 1943	UGS.4 (Hampton Rds. - Casablanca)	Oran, Feb 3, 1943
Oran, Feb 11, 1943	ET.11 (Bone - Gibraltar)	Gibraltar, Feb 13, 1943
Gibraltar, Feb 22, 1943	GUS.4 (Oran - NYC)	New York, Mar 12, 1943

Vessel	Pdt.	Tons	Built	Cargo	Notes
ALCOA BANNER (US)		5,035	1919		SAFI
ALCOA TRADER (US)		4,986	1920		CASABLANCA
AMERICAN PRESS (US)		5,131	1920		SAFI
ANNISTON CITY (US)		5,687	1921		CASABLANCA
BRALANTA (Nor)		9,608	1936		ORAN
CHARLES C PINCKNEY (US)		**7,177**	**1942**		**STRAGGLED 20.1.43**
CITY OF FLINT (US)		**4,963**	**1920**		**STRAGGLED & SUNK BY U 575**
DANIEL BOONE (US)		7,176	1942		ORAN
DANIEL CARROLL (US)		7,176	1942		CASABLANCA
EDWIN MARKHAM (US)		7,176	1942		CASABLANCA
EMPIRE GRENADIER (Br)		9,811	1942		ORAN
ESSO BAYONNE (US)		7,698	1937		GIBRALTAR
ESSO MONTPELIER (US)		**7,698**	**1940**		**ORAN**
GEORGE LEONARD (US)		7,176	1942		CASABLANCA
GREEN MOUNTAIN (US)		4,988	1919		CASABLANCA
HAWAIIAN (US)		4,868	1919		CASABLANCA
HOUSATONIC (US)		10,097	1941		
HOUSTON VOLUNTEERS (US)		7,176	1942		CASABLANCA
JAMES IREDELL (US)		7,177	1942		CASABLANCA
JOHN MCLOUGHLIN (US)		7,176	1942		CASABLANCA
JOSHUA SENEY (US)		7,176	1942		CASABLANCA
JULIA WARD HOWE (US)		**7,176**	**1942**		**STRAGGLED AND SUNK BY U 442**
KAWEAH (US)		5,450	1921		
LORD DELAWARE (US)		7,200	1942		CASABLANCA
MARSHALL ELLIOTT (US)		7,177	1942		ORAN

MIRABEAU B LAMAR (US)	7,176	1942	ORAN
NATHANIEL BACON (US)	7,176	1942	CASABLANCA
NEW ORLEANS (US)	6,172	1920	SAFI
NORLYS (Pan)	9,892	1936	ORAN
OCEAN VIGIL (Br)	7,174	1941	CASABLANCA
PEARL HARBOR (US)	7,200	1942	CASABLANCA
PHILIP LIVINGSTON (US)	7,176	1941	ORAN
POTTER (Pan)	6,174	1920	CASABLANCA
ROBIN GRAY (US)	6,896	1920	CASABLANCA
SALAMIS (Nor)	8,286	1939	ORAN
SAMUEL GRIFFIN (US)	7,176	1942	CASABLANCA
SAMUEL JOHNSTON (US)	7,191	1942	ORAN
SOLOR (Nor)	8,262	1938	CASABLANCA
THADDEUS KOSCIUSZKO (US)	7,200	1942	ORAN
THEODORIC BLAND (US)	7,176	1942	ORAN
THOMAS LYNCH (US)	7,176	1942	ORAN
THORSHOLM (Nor)	9,937	1937	ORAN
USS BENSON			ESCORT 13/01 - 02/02
USS GLEAVES			ESCORT 13/01 - 02/02
USS KENDRICK			ESCORT 13/01 - 02/02
USS MAYO			ESCORT 13/01 - 02/02
USS NIBLACK			ESCORT 13/01 - 02/02
USS PLUNKETT			ESCORT 13/01 - 02/02
VINLAND (Nor)	4,436	1924	CASABLANCA
WILLIAM C CLAIBORNE (US)	7,176	1942	ORAN
WILLIAM MOULTRIE (US)	7,177	1942	ORAN
WILLIAM P FESSENDEN (US)	7,176	1942	ORAN
ZACHARY TAYLOR (US)	7,181	1942	ORAN

(b)

F1

THIRD NAVAL DISTRICT
OFFICE OF THE PORT DIRECTOR
CONFIDENTIAL   PORT OF NEW YORK
SERIAL PDNYF 06211   DATE January 16, 1943

SUPPLEMENTARY REPORT OF SUPPLIES AND/OR PERSONNEL
ISSUED BY PORT DIRECTOR, TO:

MS
SS ESSO MONTPELIER   SAILING DATE: 1/12/43
GROSS TONS 7968 TYPE Tanker   DESTINATION: ----

ARMED GUARD PERSONNEL REMOVED

NAME	RATING	BRANCH	SERVICE NO.
HIGGINS, Kenneth E.	Lt.(jg)	USNR, D-V(S)	
KENYON, Allerton Brewster	Cox	M-2, USNR	403-96-45
BURKE, William Joseph	S2c	V-6, USNR	622-97-64
HOPPER, Lyle Thomas	S2c	V-6, USNR	611-60-87
HUMMEL, Willie Edward	S2c	USN	283-73-61
ROYAL, Robert Lee	S2c	USN	256-43-93
TRANEY, Frederick Allen	S2c	USN	258-12-26

ARMED GUARD PERSONNEL PUT ABOARD

THORNHILL, James Washington	Lt.(jg)	USNR, D-V(S)	
HODGE, Ferris Simon	BM2c	V-6, USNR	311-05-35
BRYAN, Ernest Victor	S1c	V-6, USNR	636-79-12
KINDER, Joseph William	S1c	V-6, USNR	652-94-20
KING, Edwin Earl	S1c	V-6, USNR	722-51-73
KISCADDEN, Ralph Clarence	S1c	USN	244-27-23
KOCH, John James	S1c	V-6, USNR	707-12-14

COMMUNICATION LIAISON PERSONNEL PUT ABOARD

STEVENS, Robert Elmer	RM3c	V-6, USNR	618-37-19
HEISLER, John Edward Jr.	RM3c	V-6, USNR	666-32-18

MATERIAL FURNISHED

Under Cognizance of BuOrd: None
Under Cognizance of BuShips: Per attached sheet
Report on Clothing and Publications: Per attached sheet

Copy to: OPNAV   Port Director,
         BuORD
         BuSHIPS
         BuPERS (Complies w/C.L. 27-42.)

JAN 2 1943
RECEIVED
NAVY DEPARTMENT

Figure 42. SS *Esso Montpelier* Oil Tanker Armed Guard Personnel Roster

(c)

#20

PORT DIRECTOR'S REPORT—ARMING MERCHANT VESSELS

CONFIDENTIAL
SERIAL PD _____   ARMED FOR AREA ___1A___

18X
SS ESSO MONTPELIER   GROSS TONS 7699   DEADWEIGHT TONS 11310m
WHERE
ARMED (PORT) NY, NY   DATE 3/23/43   YARD   Beth., SI

LIST ALL GUNS (INCLUDING MACHINE GUNS) ABOARD VESSEL
ON DEPARTURE.

Nr. of Guns	Caliber & Type	Gun Mark & Mod.	Mount Mk. & Mod.	Gun Location	Ammunition
*1	4"50	IX-5	XII-3	Aft	
*1	3"50	21	XXII	Fwd	
*2	20 mm	4	4	Fwd	
*2	20 mm	II	4-2	Amidship	
3	20 mm	4	4	Aft	12240
1	20 mm	II	4-2	Aft	

BuOrd form Nr.228 (rev. May 1942) submitted 4/1   1943, in triplicate
**2   .30 Lewis
*Guns and amm. prev. installed.INS
**Guns removed.

	ITEM	DETAIL
1.	Splinter Protection - Bridge	Steel and concrete
	Splinter Protection - AA Machine Guns	4 steel, 4 concrete & steel
2.	Gun foundations, number and location	10: 5 aft, 2 mid., 3 fwd
3.	Magazines, number and location	1 fwd,- ready boxes aft
4.	Painting	Gray
5.	Darkening Ship Facilities	Installed
6.	Reinforce Sea Chests	Concrete
7.	Fire Control Communication System	Installed
8.	Sky Look Out Stations, Number and Location	1 upper bridge
9.	Results Industrial Manager's Inspection	-
10.	Messing Facilities	Independent

ACCOMMODATIONS NAVY PERSONNEL

ARMED GUARD UNIT	SPACE	LOCATION
Officer in Charge	Room # 1	Amidship
Petty Officer	1	Amidship
Seamen	10	Amidship
	11	Aft

COMMUNICATION GROUP

Figure 43. Guns Aboard Vessel on Departure

Appendix II

U-565 War Diary Comments
by the FdU and the BdU
February 14 to March 5, 1943

Figure 44. German Navy submarine *U-565*.

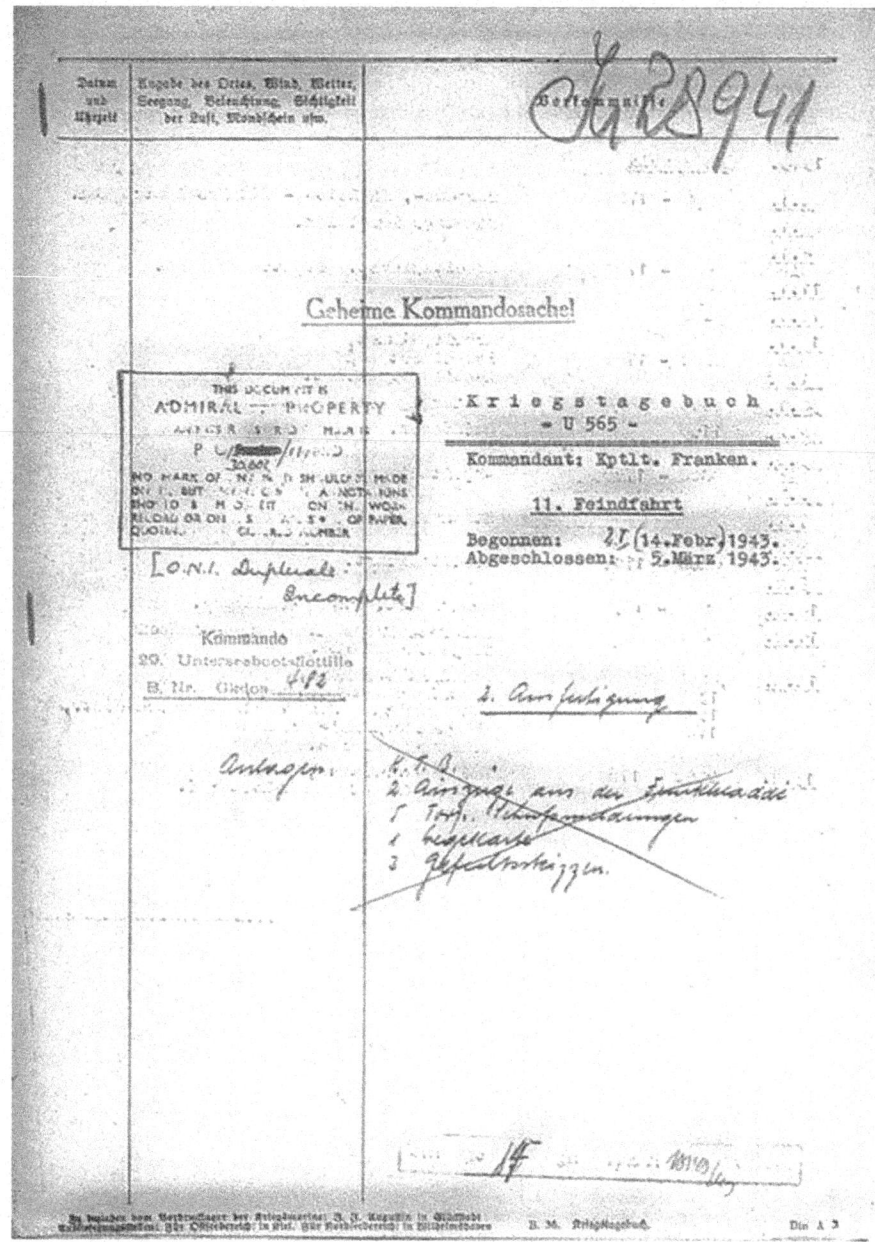

Figure 45. *U-565* – Original German War Diary (KTB) for Franken

Comments of the FdU and the BdU on the War Diary entries *U 565* (Franken) from February 14 to March 5, 1943

1) A well-executed patrol, the best testament to the proven Kommandant and his crew. The shooting opportunities were decisively exploited, and the attacks were driven home with judiciousness and guts, especially noteworthy the reloading on 27 February despite the proximity of the escort vessels, with the decision to sink the shot [damaged] tanker in any case.

2) Torpedo use:

A) 24 February.

The sinking of the steamer is accepted as certain—also, the B-Dienst [Service] talk of the rescue of survivors. [*Nathanael Greene*]

B) 27 February. [*Seminole*]

The sinking of the tanker is expected.

C) 1 March.

The fan-miss is due to incorrect estimation. [Ship Name Unknown]

3) The suspicion that there is enemy locating gear in the Balearic Islands is often expressed by Kommandant.

4) Accredited as sunk:

1 Tanker of 10,000 GRT. [*Seminole*]

1 Steamer of 8,000 GRT. [*Nathanael Greene*]

As torpedoed:

1 Freighter of 8,000 GRT.

The comments of the FdU-Italien are approved.

A very well executed patrol. The attacking spirit and the tenacity on the attack on 27 February are exemplary.

Accredited success: 2 ships = 18,000 GRT sunk and one freighter 8,000 GRT torpedoed.

For the BdU Chief of the Operations Department-

Appendix III

UGS-7 Convoy Fleet List

72 Merchants and 9 Escorts

Departures	Convoy	Arrivals
New York, Apr 2, 1943	UGS.7 (Hampton Rds. - Bone)	Algiers, Apr 21, 1943
Algiers, Apr 24, 1943	MKS.12 (Bone - r/v WITH SL 128)	Gibraltar, Apr 26, 1943
Gibraltar, May 8, 1943	GUS.7 (Passed Gibraltar - Hampton Rds.)	Hampton Roads, May 26, 1943

Vessel	Pdt.	Tons	Built	Cargo	Notes
ABBEYDALE (Br)		8,299	1937		ALGIERS
ALEXANDER HAMILTON (US)		7,191	1942		CASABLANCA
ALGIC (US)		5,496	1920		ORAN
ANNA KNUDSEN (Nor)		9,057	1931	FUEL OIL	ALGIERS
ANTONIA (Du)		3,357	1938		ALGIERS TO BONE
BENJAMIN BOURN (US)		7,176	1942		ORAN TO BONE
BERNARD CARTER (US)		7,191	1942		ORAN
BRAJARA (Nor)		8,116	1934		ORAN
CHARLES H CRAMP (US)		6,220	1920		ORAN
DANIEL HUGER (US)		7,176	1942		ALGIERS
DAVID G FARRAGUT (US)		7,191	1942		ALGIERS
DELNORTE (US)		4,982	1919		ORAN
DJEBEL AURES (Fr)		2,835	1929		GIB TO ORAN
EDWIN MARKHAM (US)		7,176	1942		ALGIERS
EMPIRE BAIRN (Br)		813	1941		ALGIERS TO BONE

EMPIRE CAMERON (Br)	7,015	1941		ALGIERS TO PHILIPEVILLE
EMPIRE COBBETT (Br)	9,811	1942		CASABLANCA
EMPIRE FLETCHER (Br)	8,194	1942		ALGIERS
EMPIRE GOLD (Br)	8,028	1941		GIB TO ALGIERS
ENOREE (US)	10,180	1942	USN OILER	ESCORT OILER, CASABLANCA
ESSO MONTPELIER (US)	**7,698**	**1940**		**ALGIERS**
EXILONA (US)	4,971	1919		RETURNED
GEORGE LEONARD (US)	7,176	1942		RETURNED
GEORGE SHIRAS (US)	7,200	1943		GIB TO PHILIPEVILLE
GIDEON WELLES (US)	7,176	1942		ORAN
GREEN MOUNTAIN (US)	4,988	1919		ALGIERS
GULF OF MEXICO (US)	7,807	1917		ORAN
HENRY W LONGFELLOW (US)	7,176	1942		CASABLANCA TO BONE
HORACE BINNEY (US)	7,191	1942		RETURNED
HOUSTON VOLUNTEERS (US)	7,176	1942		ALGIERS
JAMES MOORE (US)	7,177	1943		CASABLANCA
JAMES W DENVER (US)	**7,200**	**1943**		**SUNK BY U 195**
JOHN DICKINSON (US)	7,176	1942		CASABLANCA
JOHN P POE (US)	7,191	1942		ORAN

JOHN SERGEANT (US)		7,191	1942	ORAN
JOHN TRUMBULL (US)		7,176	1943	ORAN
JOSEPH N TEAL (US)		7,176	1942	CASABLANCA
LELAND STANFORD (US)		7,276	1942	ORAN
LORRAINE (Fr)		9,809	1937	ORAN
LST 364				ORAN TO PHILIPEVILLE
LST 367				ORAN TO BOUGIE
LST 407				ORAN TO BOUGIE
LST 409				ORAN TO PHILIPEVILLE
LST 413				ORAN TO BOUGIE
MARK TWAIN (US)		7,176	1942	ORAN
MARS (Du)		1,582	1925	ALGIERS TO BOUGIE
MARSHALL ELLIOTT (US)		7,177	1942	ORAN
MEROPE (Du)		1,162	1918	ORAN TO PHILIPEVILLE
MICHIGAN (US)	**81**	**5,594**	**1919**	**SUNK BY U 565**
MIRABEAU B LAMAR (US)		7,176	1942	RETURNED
NATHANIEL BACON (US)		7,176	1942	ALGIERS
NEW ORLEANS (US)		6,172	1920	ORAN
OCEAN VIGIL (Br)		7,174	1941	ALGIERS TO PHILIPEVILLE
PAT HARRISON (US)		7,191	1943	ORAN
PEARL HARBOR (US)		7,200	1942	ORAN
POLARTANK (Nor)		6,356	1930	ORAN

REVERDY JOHNSON (US)	7,191	1942		RETURNED
RICHARD JORDAN GATLING (US)	7,181	1942		GIB TO PHILIPEVILLE
SIDI-BEL-ABBES (Fr)	**4,392**	**1929**		**1131 TROOPS. SUNK BY U 565.VIA CASABLANCA**
SIDI-BRAHIM (Br)	2,439	1910		GIB TO ORAN
THADDEUS KOSCIUSZKO (US)	7,200	1942		ORAN
THOMAS B ROBERTSON (US)	7,176	1942		
THOMAS LYNCH (US)	7,176	1942		ORAN
THOMAS PINCKNEY (US)	7,177	1942		RETURNED
THOMAS STONE (US)	7,191	1942		
TIDE WATER (US)	8,886	1930		GIBRALTAR
USS CHARLES AUSBURNE				ESCORT 01/04 - 22/04
USS CLAXTON				ESCORT 01/04 - 22/04
USS FOOTE				ESCORT 01/04 - 22/04
USS RINGGOLD				ESCORT 01/04 - 22/04
USS SCHROEDER				ESCORT 01/04 - 22/04
USS SPENCE				ESCORT 01/04 - 22/04
USS STEVENSON				ESCORT 01/04 - 22/04
USS STOCKTON				ESCORT 01/04 - 22/04

VILLE DE DJIDJELLI (Fr)	1,132	1907		ORAN TO BOUGIE
WILLIAM BREWSTER (US)	7,176	1942		PUT BACK
WILLIAM D MOSELEY (US)	7,177	1943		CASABLANCA
WILLIAM H SEWARD (US)	7,176	1942		ORAN
WILLIAM JOHNSON (US)	7,191	1942		GIB TO PHILIPEVILLE
WILLIAM TILGIIMAN (US)	7,191	1942		RETURNED
ZACHARY TAYLOR (US)	7,181	1942		ORAN

Appendix IV

Translated War Diary Patrol Report of KptLt. Franken

April 19 to April 21, 1943

Intercepted Enemy Radio Traffic – *U-565*

Date and Time	Position, Wind, Weather, Sea state, Lighting, Visibility, Moonlight, etc.	Events
19.04.43	South of Spain	
20.00	CH 7732	
21.18		Radio Message from B.d.U.:
		West Boats: From Agent report passed Ceuta about
		12.00 hours course for the Mediterranean
		2-transports
		32-freighters
		6-tankers
		9-escort units.
	CH 7498	Surfaced.
	CH 7498	Course 340°
	CH 7498	The reported convoy is in sight bearing 310°T. Range 10,000 meters. [about 6.2 miles] At the front escort vessels, among them a large destroyer, which zig-zags at high speed in large legs ahead of the formation. Fu.M.G. in use. [presumably escort's radar]

		Radio Message sent:
20.04.43		22.10 hours eastbound convoy naval square CH 7488, course
00.00	CH 7579	90°, 10 knots. -*Franken*-
	NE 0-1, Sea 1, Vis. Good, bright moonshine	
	Northwest of the Gulf of Oran	
01.10	CH 7588	
04.00	CH 7679	
	SE 2-3, Sea 2, individual clouds, Vis. Good	Course 90°
04.33	CH7687	
04.45	CH7687	
		Radio Message from F.d.U., [U-boat Command, Italy]by which
04.58	CH 7687	the convoy was seen of Alboran Island at 23.45 hours
		Dived.
06.30	CH 7684	The sound bearing of the convoy is 290°T.
		Course 45°

			To Action Stations!
			I was forced off by the escorting destroyer—steered evasion courses. In the very good visibility – it is the full moon night, lightly cloudy – there is no prospect of getting into shooting position. So as not to waste time unnecessarily, because the convoy runs at 10 knots and I can also be detected at any time by the radar, I decide to refrain from further attempts at attack and to run ahead to attack submerged in the early morning twilight.
			I can allow myself this speculation in this sea area, as the experience of the previous war patrols has shown, I can determine the approach of the convoy precisely. According to my calculation, this time, it must pass through CH 7685. He cannot go south because of the proximity to the coast, and he will not evade to the north for reasons of time-saving. With a 2 hour lead, I am always able to reach a favorable shooting position with the help of the listening gear.
			While maneuvering ahead, observed intense speech and radio traffic on the convoy voice wavelength (124.5) meters). Several times the call-sign "Melbourne," presumably the name of a steamer.

		To Action Stations!
06.36		Twilight. The convoy is still not seen. However, the sound
06.42		bearing has grown so that I expect it to be in sight at lightness.
06.57		Explosive locating and Asdic gear are heard.
07.23	CH 7687	Course 50°
	Sea 1, hazy horizon.	Course 80°
		Course 50°
		Convoy in sight bearing 300°T.
		On a course of 50° and medium speed, I close up well on the
		flank. The leading, locating destroyer group has not picked me
		up. The convoy proceeds in 3 columns. The most valuable
07.46		steamers in the center. I reach a shooting position on the middle
		column and am positioned in the convoy between the center
		and the starboard columns.
		Shot from Tube I on a loaded 6000 CRT freighter. [*Michigan*]
20.04.43	West of the Gulf of Oran	Enemy speed 10 knots,
		Target angle right 95°
		Range 400 meters,
		Lead angle 19°,
		Shooting angle 305°,
		Depth 4 meters,
		Pi G 7 H

07.57			Hit aft 20 meters after 15 seconds, running track 200 meters. High explosion column. After mast buckles. The aft rudder cabin flies high into the air, as well as the lifeboat and other ship cargo pieces. Steamer stops and settles deeper quickly aft. Ammunition stowed in the aft cargo hatch detonate one after another in small, however ongoing detonations. Steamer settles deeper. In the meantime, the next group comes into shooting position. 2-fan from tubes II and III on a large troop transport, [*Sidi-bel-Abbes*] two smokestack passenger ship. Minimum 12000GRT, if not more. Apparently, the convoy leader is on board because several flag signals were issued. Enemy speed 10 knots, Target angle right 113°, Range 1000 meters, Lead angle 18°, Spread angle 4°, Shooting angle 336°, Depth 7 meters, Pi 2 MZ-on.

		After 31 and 33 seconds, running track 500 meters, 2 hits forward 50 meters and center. The 2nd torpedo did not go high order because of the detonation of the first but also hit the target. Enormous detonation. Red fiery glow, sheet of flame, black explosion column. Because of this, the transport is completely covered; one can see only the buckling masts. After that, I see the transport [*Sidi-bel-Abbes*] already low in the water with a strong starboard list. It settles deeper and heels over. It is irretrievable lost. Now I want to get a big tanker with tube V. [*Esso Montpelier*] However, the tanker obviously saw my periscope. He turns from target angle 40°, range 300 meters, exactly towards me. So as not to be rammed went to depth 40 meters. Strong sinking sounds of the troop transport breaking apart. In between still heard, the continual small steamer torpedoed first.
08.05	CH 7679	
08.30	CH 7679	

09.57		In the meantime, the convoy has come alive We are approached by a locating destroyer- to depth A +40 meters. Destroyer overran us.
10.55	CH 7682	
		Course 20°
12.00	CH 7681	
		Silent running. 2 corvettes remain in the vicinity.
16.00	CH 7648	Steered avoiding courses.
20.00	CH 7645	
21.26	CH 7645	Strong sinking sounds. Obviously, the steamer torpedoed first.
21.29	CH 7645	Then the smaller detonations stopped too.
22.01	Ch 7642	
22.05	Ch 7642	Move off on course 315°.
23.10		
		Day's run: 97.5 nm
		30.47 nm = 127.97 nm
		Surfaced.
		Crash dive for aircraft detection, depth A-20 meters.
21.04.43		Surfaced.
	CH 7296	Course 340°
00.25		Radio Message to F.d.U.:

		07.52 hours naval square CH 7682 from eastbound convoy: 1.) Troop transport (2-smokestack passenger ship) 12000GRT, 2 MZ. 2.) One freighter with ammunition, 6000 GRT. Toneless aircraft detection 170 cm. - *Franken* – Radio Message from F.d.U.: [U-boat Command, Italy] To *Franken*: Bravo!

Figure 46. Translated War Diary Patrol Report of KptLt. Franken on *U-565* for April 19 to April 21, 1943

Appendix V

Handwritten Journal of
Armed Guard S/1C Ernest Bryan
April 19 to April 21, 1943

#8.

Monday 19, 1943
Mediterranien

Passed the Rock of Gibraltar around nine
oclock this morning the weather was
a little hazy but now it is beautiful.
Tonight we have a full moon and it
sure does make me homesick. I have been
playing a little poker and quit about
ninety cents winner. I mounted the sights
on all 20 m.m. guns to-day and am now
ready for the planes. Bad news to-night
it looks as if we are going to Malta,
the captain thinks so too. Well if we
do I hope we can at least deliver
our cargo so it can do some good over
here even if we don't get back ourselves.
I love you darling with all my heart.

Tuesday 20, 1943
Mediterranien

I was awakened at ten minutes of eight this
morning by an explosion from a torpedo. The
French troop ship "Sidi Bel Abbis" loaded with
troops had been hit amidships and it almost

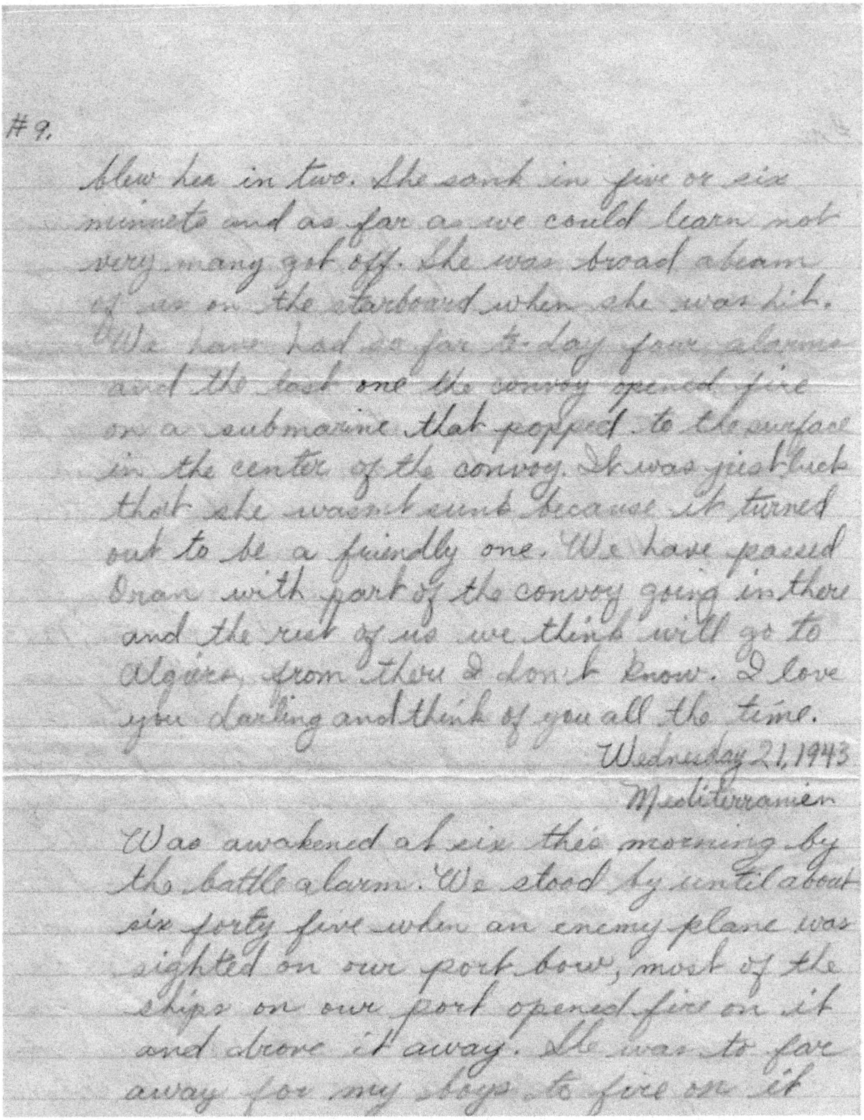

#9.

blew her in two. She sank in five or six minutes and as far as we could learn not very many got off. She was broad abeam of us on the starboard when she was hit. We have had so far to-day four alarms and the last one the convoy opened fire on a submarine that popped to the surface in the center of the convoy. It was just luck that she wasn't sunk because it turned out to be a friendly one. We have passed Oran with part of the convoy going in there and the rest of us we think will go to Algiers, from there I don't know. I love you darling and think of you all the time.

Wednesday 21, 1943

Mediterranean

Was awakened at six this morning by the battle alarm. We stood by until about six forty five when an enemy plane was sighted on our port bow, most of the ships on our port opened fire on it and drove it away. She was to far away for my boys to fire on it

Figure 47. Handwritten journal of Armed Guard S/1C Ernest Bryan.

Appendix VI

HX-242 Convoy Fleet List

64 Merchants and 29 Escorts

Departure	Convoy	Arrival
New York, May 31, 1943	HX-242 (NYC - Liverpool)	Clyde, Jun 15, 1943
Clyde, Jun 16, 1943	ON-189 (Liverpool - NYC)	New York, Jul 1, 1943

Vessel	Pdt.	Tons	Built	Cargo	Notes
AALSUM (Du)	42	5,418	1922	GENERAL, EXPL	
AGASSIZ					ESCORT 06/06 - 14/06
ANTAR (Br)	115	5,222	1941	STEEL, GENERAL	
ASKEPOT (Nor)	21	1,312	1937	STORES	ST JOHN NF
AXTELL J BYLES (US)	131	9,059	1927	PETROL	
BAYANO (Br)	76	6,815	1917	FRIG, METAL EX HALIFAX	
BEAVERHILL (Br)	92	10,041	1928	GENERAL EX HALIFAX	
BITER					ESCORT 09/06 - 12/06
BRAJARA (Nor)	54	8,116	1934	FFO	
BRITISH FORTITUDE (Br)	123	8,482	1937	PETROL	
BRITISH RESOLUTION (Br)	111	8,408	1937	PETROL	
BURWELL					ESCORT 06/06 - 14/06
CAIRNVALONA (Br)	62	4,929	1918	FRIG, GENERAL	

CHESAPEAKE (Br)	72	8,955	1928	FFO	ESCORT OILER
CLAVELLA (Du)	73	8,097	1939	FUEL OIL	
CONTRACTOR (Br)	35	6,004	1930	GRAIN EX HALIFAX	
DAGEID (Nor)	65	6,361	1931	GAS OIL	
DAVID G BURNET (US)	142	7,244	1943	SULPHUR, GENERAL	fitted with AND
DEWSBURY (Br)	96	1,686	1910		RESCUE SHIP
EMILY DICKINSON (US)	24	7,176	1943	GENERAL EX HALIFAX	RETURNED
EMPIRE BOMBARDIER (Br)	102	8,202	1943	ALCOHOL, PETROL	fitted with AND
EMPIRE BRUTUS (Br)	141	7,233	1943	STEEL GENERAL	fitted with AND
EMPIRE CELIA (Br)	55	7,025	1943	STEEL, LUMBER	fitted with AND
EMPIRE DICKENS (Br)	93	9,819	1942	PETROL	
EMPIRE FAITH (Br)	12	7,061	1941	GRAIN, AFVs EX HALIFAX	
EMPIRE FLETCHER (Br)	64	8,194	1942	PETROL	
EMPIRE MIST (Br)	75	7,241	1941	GENERAL	
ESSO BELGIUM (Bel)		10,568	1937		HALIFAX
ESSO DOVER (US)	132	8,880	1921	FUEL OIL	

ESSO MONTPELIER (US)	**41**	**7,698**	**1940**	**FFO**	
FENNEL					ESCORT 31/05 - 03/06
FORT CONNOLLY (Br)	34	7,133	1943	METAL, GRAIN, LUMBER	
FORT ENTERPRISE (Br)	91	7,126	1943	LUMBER, METAL	
FORT MAISONNEUVE (Br)	11	7,128	1942	GENERAL, GRAIN EX HALIFAX	
FORT MINGAN (Br)	144	7,130	1943	GRAIN, MT, EX HALIFAX	fitted with AND. PUT BACK
FORT SOURIS (Br)	23	7,134	1942	GRAIN	fitted with AND
FORT VERCHERES (Br)	151	7,128	1942	GRAIN, GENERAL EX HALIFAX	fitted with AND
FORT WRIGLEY (Br)	124	7,128	1943	GENERAL	
G HARRISON SMITH (US)	121	11,752	1930	PETROL	
GALT					ESCORT 06/06 - 14/06
GEFION (Nor)	103	9,475	1938	PETROL	
GLACIER PARK (Br)	143	7,137	1943	GRAIN, GENERAL, EXPL EX HALIFAX	fitted with AND
GULFPOINT (US)	33	6,972	1920	USN FUEL	

HENRY S FOOTE (US)	113	7,176	1943	AMMO, GENERAL	
HERANGER (Nor)	95	4,877	1930	GENERAL, EXPL	
HOPEMOUNT (Br)	32	7,434	1929	FFO	ESCORT OILER
ITCHEN					ESCORT 06/06 - 14/06
JAMAICA PLANTER (Br)	134	4,098	1936	GENERAL EX HALIFAX	INDEP EX B LOUGH AREA
JAMES J PETTIGREW (US)	45	7,177	1942	GENERAL EX HALIFAX	
JED					ESCORT 09/06 - 12/06
JOHN A BROWN (Br)	114	10,455	1938	PETROL	HIT ICEBERG 5.6 IN 45.04N 48.33W
JOHN DRAKE SLOAT (US)	133	7,176	1943	GENERAL	
JOHN P HOLLAND (US)	74	7,176	1942	AMMO, GENERAL	
JUBAL A EARLY (US)	43	7,244	1943	SUGAR	
KITCHENER					ESCORT 04/06 - 06/06
L ABSHIRE (US)		6,353	1917		HALIFAX
LACHINE					ESCORT 31/05 - 06/06
LAURELWOOD (Br)	82	7,347	1929	FFO	ESCORT OILER
MAYA (Hon)	63	5,523	1929	EXPL, GENERAL, FRIG	

MELAMPUS (Du)	66	5,962	1924	GENERAL, EX HALIFAX	
MONTGOMERY					ESCORT 31/05 - 06/06
NANAIMO					ESCORT 31/05 - 03/06
NEWBROUGH (Br)	152	5,255	1941	GRAIN, MT	
NICANIA (Br)	112	8,179	1942	PETROL fitted with AND	RETURNED WITH ICE DAMAGE
NORANDA					ESCORT 31/05 - 03/06
NOREG (Nor)	53	7,605	1931	FFO	ESCORT OILER
NORSOL (Nor)	104	8,236	1941	AVGAS	
OREGON EXPRESS (Nor)	71	3,642	1933	FRIG, GENERAL	RETURNED
ORWELL (Nor)	44	7,920	1905	FFO	ESCORT OILER
PAN-MAINE (US)	52	7,237	1936	GAS OIL	
PANDORIAN (Br)	13	4,159	1941	GENERAL EX HALIFAX	
PAUL H HARWOOD (US)	61	6,610	1918	VAP OIL	
PELICAN					ESCORT 09/06 - 12/06
PETER CARTWRIGHT (US)	135	7,176	1942	GENERAL	
POLARTANK (Nor)	31	6,356	1930	VAP OIL	
PORT ARTHUR					ESCORT 04/06 - 06/06

REGINA					ESCORT 03/06 - 06/06
SACKVILLE					ESCORT 06/06 - 14/06
SAN ELISEO (Br)	105	8,042	1939	PARAFFIN	
SKIENSFJORD (Nor)	101	5,922	1922	EXPL, GENERAL	
SPEY					ESCORT 09/06 - 12/06
ST ALBANS					ESCORT 03/06 - 06/06
ST FRANCIS					ESCORT 06/06 - 14/06
ST LAURENT					ESCORT 06/06 - 14/06
THOMAS NELSON (US)	94	7,191	1942	STORES, EXPL	
THORSHOV (Nor)	122	9,955	1935	PETROL	
TIMMINS					ESCORT 03/06 - 06/06
TORTUGUERO (Br)	81	5,285	1921	FRIG	
TRAIL					ESCORT 03/06 - 06/06
TYNDAREUS (Br)	51	11,361	1916	GENERAL	
WEAR					ESCORT 09/06 - 12/06
WILLIAM MCKINLEY (US)	22	7,200	1943	WHEAT, STEEL	
WOODSTOCK					ESCORT 04/06 - 06/06

Appendix VII

Comments of the FdU Italien on the
War Diary of *U-565*
March 6 to May 12, 1943

1) An excellently executed patrol, which placed very high demands on the Kommandant and crew.

2) On attacks carried out and use of the torpedo armament is noted:

> a) The operation on the convoy on 19/20 April, deserves special recognition. The decision of the Kommandant to initially give up the attack in the bright full moon night and maneuver ahead for submerged day attack despite hostile locating in the sharply monitored sea area was bold; the unwavering will to succeed, excellent tactical understanding, confidence in himself and the crew, were decisive for the success. The attack brought on the next morning by the screen at close range to the valuable targets was carried out excellently. A prime example of a fresh, daring, prudent, and skillful U-boat attack.

> b) In the attack on the tanker convoy on 1 May, the use of a four-fan was justified despite the long distance, which was presumably considerably underestimated at 3,000 meters. There is a high probability that a hit was achieved.

> c) With the fan on 8 May, in addition to speed estimation, it is also possible to underestimate the distance and thus to be able to shoot out of range at a broad target angle.

3) The observation and conjecture concerning enemy locating activity

> a) by enemy units in the Balearic Islands.

> b) by two aircraft working together with tone and toneless locating.

> c) by hospital ship with toneless locating provides valuable information.

4) The clean, accurate, and concise direction of KTB deserves recognition.

5) Accredited were:

a) Sank: One troop transport of 12,000 GRT

One steamer of 6,000 GRT.

b) Torpedoes: One tanker of 12,000 GRT.

Comments of the Befehlshabers der Unterseeboote on the KTB "U-565" (Franken)

There is nothing to add to the comments of the FdU.

For the BdU Chief of the Operations Department-

Appendix VIII

North Atlantic and Mid-Atlantic Convoy Routing

The convoy sea routes traveled by the US Navy and Merchant Marines included the North and South Atlantic Ocean, the Pacific Ocean, the Indian Ocean, the Mediterranean Sea, and the deadly Arctic Ocean (Murmansk Run, Russia) route to the Soviet Union. In total, as many as 10,000 merchant ships traveled the seas during the war. These ships, mostly tankers and freighters, also included passenger liners transformed into troop transports.

The number of North Atlantic and Mid-Atlantic convoys alone and their fleet numbers remained high from 1942 through 1943, increasing in 1944 while traveling their designated routes. Although, after the U-boat campaign halted during "Black May" of 1943, the numbers in the charts below clearly show the decrease in ship loss and damages in 1944 and 1945 for the Atlantic Trade Convoys, UGF, UGS, OT, UT, CU, and AT convoys.

PRINCIPAL NORTH ATLANTIC AND MID ATLANTIC CONVOYS [a]

| | | | | | | Casualties (Enemy Action) [c] | | |
Arriving	Convoys	Ships	Ships per Convoy	Escorts	Escorts per Convoy	Sunk in Convoy	Sunk as Straggler	Damaged
1942	253	7,882	31	1,547	6.1	127	39	17
1943	299	12,745	43	2,481	8.3	126	49	20
1944	380	18,856	50	3,070	8.1	15	3	11
1945[b]	202	8,514	42	1,135	5.6	7	0	5
Total	**1,134**	**47,997**	--	**8,233**	**7.3**	**275**	**91**	**53**

(a) North Atlantic Trade Convoys, UGF, **UGS**, OT, UT, CU, and AT convoys and returning counterparts, ..., plus certain other important convoys, as published in the yearly convoy summaries appearing in *U. S. Fleet Anti-Submarine Bulletins*. (b) Sailing prior to VE Day(c) Including escorts.

Source: History of Convoy and Routing, United States Naval Administration in WWII, Ocean Convoys, Chapter 3, 31, http://www.ibiblio.org/hyperwar/USN/Admin-Hist/011-Convoy/.

Glossary of Navy Terms

Abeam: Behind, toward the stern.

Action Stations: German U-boat preassigned places within the U-boat where crew members work during engagements with the enemy.

Aft: Toward or in the rearmost section of a ship.

Amidships: Toward or in the middle portion of a vessel.

Astern: Toward or in a position or location behind the ship or at the stern.

Ballast: Provides adequate stability to a vessel at sea when it is not carrying cargo. Ballast with little or no value, such as water, is pumped into tanks for weight to keep the vessel upright, weigh the ship down, and lower its center of gravity. Insufficiently ballasted boats tend to tip or heel excessively in high winds.

Battle Stations: US Navy preassigned places throughout the ship where crew members work during engagements with the enemy.

Befehlshaber der U-Boote (BdU): The title of the commander-in-chief of German submarine fleets in World War II. The term also referred to the Command Headquarters of the German U-boat command in Kiel.

Boatswain's Mate BM/Coxswain (Cox): Handles rope, wire, and anchor chain. Steers ship and charts courses. Boatswain's mates perform almost any task in connection with deck maintenance, small boat operations, navigation, and supervising all US Navy personnel assigned to a ship.

Beam: Measured dimension of a ship at its widest part.

Bow: The front of a vessel. Either side of the front (or bow) of the vessel, i.e., the port bow and starboard bow.

Commodore (Cmdre): Commodore was the title of a civilian seaman put in charge of a merchant ship in the British convoys used during World War II. Usually, the convoy commodore was a retired naval officer or a senior merchant captain drawn from the Royal Naval Reserve and aboard one of the merchant ships.

Convoy: A group of ships or vehicles traveling together, typically accompanied by armed troops, warships, or means of protection in wartime.

Corvette: A small British warship. Roughly half of the convoy escorts in the North Atlantic were corvettes.

Coup de grâce: A French term for a death blow to end the suffering of the mortally wounded.

Cutters: The collective term for US Coast Guard ships.

Depth Charge: Explosive device projected or dropped from air or surface craft and detonated at predetermined depths under water by a hydrostatic mechanism.

Destroyer: Fast, maneuverable, long-endurance warship intended to escort larger vessels in a fleet, convoy, or battle group and to defend them against powerful short-range attackers.

Destroyer Escort: Warship optimized for anti-submarine warfare, having a tighter turning radius and more specialized armament than fleet destroyers. Over 500 destroyer escorts were commissioned from 1943 to 1945 and became formidable U-boat hunters.

Escort: A ship or aircraft used to protect merchant ships, warships, or convoys.

Flotilla, 29th U-boat: Formed in December 1941 in La Spezia in Italy. The flotilla primarily operated various marks of the Type VII U-boat, and it concentrated its efforts mainly in the Mediterranean Sea against Allied convoys. *U-boat 565* was under the 29th Flotilla command. In August 1943, the flotilla moved to Toulon, France, but also had U-boats in Marseille, France, and Salamis, Greece.

Führer der Unterseeboote (FdU): Officer of U-boat command, Italy. The first U-boat region was created in Italy in November 1941 to provide local command authority for the U-boat flotillas operating in the Mediterranean Sea.

Hawse/Hawser: A nautical term for a thick cable or rope used in mooring or towing a ship. Also, the arrangement of a ship's anchor cables when both starboard and port anchors are secured.

Heeling: A temporary inclination of a ship, caused by outside forces such as winds, waves, or a ship's turn.

HX: The designation for a convoy route that carried traffic from Halifax, Nova Scotia, to Liverpool, England.

Knot: A unit of speed, equaling one nautical mile per hour.

Kriegstagebuch (KTB): The official German after-action reports, logbooks, and combat diaries that were maintained by units in the field.

Liberty Ship: A class of cargo ships, built for its simple, low-cost "emergency" type of construction by the US Maritime Commission in World War II. Liberty ships were nicknamed "ugly ducklings" by President Franklin Delano Roosevelt. Nearly 3,000 were mass-produced in less than five years from 1941 to 1945 and across seventeen different shipyards in eleven states. The largest construction sites were in California, Maryland, Oregon, Maine, Texas, and Florida.

Limpet mine: A type of naval mine attached underwater by a swimmer or diver to a target by magnets. It is so named because of its superficial similarity to the limpet, a type of sea snail that clings tightly to rocks or other hard surfaces. Usually, limpet mines are set off by time fuses.

Maritime: Connected with the sea, especially concerning seafaring commercial or military activity.

Merchant Marine (Seaman): The Merchant Marine is a fleet of ships providing transport services. In wartime, they were an auxiliary naval service, called upon to move troops, equipment, and supplies. The seamen of the merchant ships were civilian volunteers.

Navy (US) Armed Guard: A specialized service branch of the US Navy responsible for defending US and Allied merchant ships from attack by enemy aircraft, submarines, and surface ships during World War II.

Navy (US) Enlisted Military Ratings/Pay Grades

The rank or pay grade of an enlisted sailor was known as a rate.

Seaman Recruit S3c/E-1

Seaman Apprentice S2c /E-2

Seaman S1c/E-3

Boatswain/Coxswain (instead of BM3c)

Petty Officer Coxswain COX/E-4

Petty Officer BM2c/E-5

Petty Officer BM1c/E-6

Chief Petty Officer CQM/E-7

Senior Chief Petty Officer SCPO/E-8

Navy (US and German) Officers' Equivalent Ranks: *Source: Military Intelligence Division (1945). "Chapter IX," Handbook on German Military Forces. United States Department of War. Retrieved July 2020.*

US	Germany
Captain	Kapitän zur See (KzS)
Commander	Fregattenkapitän (FKpt)
Lieutenant Commander	Korvettenkapitän (KKpt)
Lieutenant	Kapitänleutnant (KptLt)
Lieutenant (Junior Grade)	Oberleutnant zur See (Oblt zS)
Ensign	Leutnant zur See (Lt zS or LZS)

On Watch/Standing Watch: A sailor's assigned period for being on duty and responsible for alerting the crew to any danger while on board ship.

Operation Neuland (New Land): The German Navy code name for the extension of Operation Paukenschlag (Drumbeat). Operation Neuland launched a second wave of attacks after Operation Drumbeat into the Caribbean Sea until August 1942 and was masterminded by Admiral Karl Dönitz in December 1941.

Periscope: An optical instrument that allowed the crews on board submarines to view activity on or above the ocean's surface while the submarine remained submerged.

Pinging: Distinctive underwater sound generated by an active sonar system on board surface vessels while searching for enemy submarines.

Port: The left side of a ship relative to someone who is facing forward toward the bow.

Scuttle: To sink one's ship deliberately by holing it or opening its seacocks to let water in.

Starboard: Right side of a ship relative to a person who is facing forward toward the bow.

Steamship (SS)/Steamer: A term used to differentiate a ship powered by steam from a ship under sail. The more specific term would be "freighter," "tanker," or "troopship."

Stem: The extreme forward line of the bow and the extension of the keel to the bow of a ship.

Stern: The rear section of a ship or the tail of a submarine.

Theater of Operations: Defined in American field manuals as the land-sea areas to be invaded or defended, including areas necessary for administrative personnel necessary to the military operations.

U-boats (Unterseeboote): "Under sea boat." Abbreviated name for German submarines.

UGS: Convoy route designation for "United States-Gibraltar Slow" in the Central Atlantic and Mediterranean.

BIBLIOGRAPHY

BBC News. "President Roosevelt Proclaims Neutrality," September 1, 1999. http://news.bbc.co.uk/2/hi/special_report/1999/08/99/world_war_ii/430187.stm.

Blair, Clay. *Hitler's U-boat War: Vol. I, The Hunters, 1939-1942*. New York: Random House, 1996.

——. *Hitler's U-boat War: Vol. II, The Hunted, 1942–1945*. New York: Random House, 1998.

Bunker, John. *Liberty Ships: The Ugly Ducklings of World War II*. Salem: Ayer Company Publishers, Inc., 1972.

Busch, R., and Hans-Joachim Roll. *German U-boat Commanders of World War II*. London: Greenhill Books, 1999.

Carlson, Ron. "U.S. Navy Armed Guard and U.S. Merchant Marine in World War II." The US Navy Armed Guard website. Accessed June 20, 2018. https://www.armed-guard.com/about-ag.html.

Churchill, Winston S. *The Second World War, Volume 2: Their Finest Hour*. London: Cassell, 1949.

——. *The Second World War: Closing the Ring*. Boston: Houghton Mifflin Company, 1951.

Clancey, Patrick, and Otto Torriero. *Arming of Merchant Ships and Naval Armed Guard*. Office of Naval Operations. Accessed July 10, 2018. https://www.ibiblio.org/hyperwar/USN/Admin-Hist/011-Convoy/index.html.

Cleave, Captain Edward C., USNR. *History of the Naval Armed Guard Afloat-World War II, OP-414,* "Chapter VI. The Battle for North Africa." Office of Naval Operations.

http://www.ibiblio.org/hyperwar/USN/Admin-Hist/011-Convoy/index.html.

Corder, Russell, "Hazardous Duty with the Naval Armed Guard." Warfare History Network website. Accessed October 17, 2018. https://warfarehistorynetwork.com/daily/wwii/hazardous-duty-with-the-naval-armed-guard/.

D'Este, Carlo. *World War II in the Mediterranean, 1942-1945.* Chapel Hill: Algonquin Books of Chapel Hill, 1990.

Forester, C.S. *The Good Shepherd.* Kingsport: Kingsport Press, Inc., 1955.

Gannon, Michael. *Black May.* 1st ed. New York: Harper Collins Publishers, Inc., 1998.

——. *Operation Drumbeat: The Dramatic True Story of Germany's First U-Boat Attacks Along the American Coast in World II.* New York: Harper & Row Publishers, 1990.

German Navy: The High Command. *The U-boat Commanders' Handbook.* (*U-Boot Kommandanten Handbuch.* Berlin, 1942). Gettysburg: Thomas Publications, 1989.

German U-boat War Diaries ("Kriegstagebuch U-565"). Secret Command Document. National Archives and Records Administration at College Park, Maryland.

Gleichauf, Justin F. *Unsung Sailors: The Naval Armed Guard in World War II.* Annapolis: US Naval Institute Press, 1990.

Grunberger, Richard. *Germany 1918-1945.* London and Norwich: B.T. Batsford Ltd, 1964.

Hague, Arnold. *The Allied Convoy System 1939-1945, Its Organization, Defence, and Operation.* Annapolis: US Naval Institute Press, 2000.

Hall, Richard C. *Consumed by War: European Conflict in the 20th Century.* Lexington: University Press of Kentucky, 2010.

Hastings, Max. *Inferno: The World at War, 1939-1945*. New York: Alfred A Knoph, 2011.

Helgason, Gudmundur. "All Convoys Hit by U-boats." Uboat.net website. Accessed October 20, 2017. http://uboat.net/ops/convoys/convoys. php?convoy=UGS-4.

Jacksch, Helmut. *U 565: Das Boot Und Seine Menschen*. (*U 565: The Boat and its People*), Jürgen A. Kraxenberger, ed., self-pub., n.d.

Kaplan, Philip, and Jack Currie. *Convoy: Merchant Sailors at War 1939-1945*. Annapolis: US Naval Institute Press, 1998.

Keith, Don. *War Beneath the Waves*. New American Library, 2010.

Kurowski, Franz. *Knight's Cross Holders of the U-Boat Service*. Atglen: Schiffer Publishing Ltd., 1995.

Kent, Francis. *The Way It Was. Naval Armed Guard WWII, The Sailors Nobody Knew*. https://www.armed-guard.com/fkent01.html. 2015.

Mackenzie, Gregory. "US Navy Armed Guard Service in WW2." Ahoy - Mac's Web Log website. Accessed July 10, 2017. http://www.ahoy.tk-jk.net/ macslog/USNavyArmedGuardServicein.html.

McCarten, Anthony. *Darkest Hour: How Churchill Brought England Back from the Brink*. New York: Harper Collins Publishers, 2017.

Miller, David. *U-Boats: The Illustrated History of the Raiders of the Deep*. Washington: Brassey's Inc, 2000.

Morison, Samuel E. *The Battle of the Atlantic 1939-1943: Volume I of History of United States Naval Operations in World War II*. Boston: Little, Brown and Company, 1966.

New England Historical Society website. "U-Boat Attacks of World War II: 6 Months of Secret Terror in the Atlantic." Accessed August 20, 2017. http://newenglandhistoricalsociety.com/u-boat-attacks-of-world-war-ii.

Naval History and Heritage Command website. National Museum of the U.S. Navy. Accessed September 9, 2018. https://www.history.navy.mil/ content/history/museums/nmusn/explore/photography/wwii/wwii-atlantic/battle-of-the-atlantic/atlantic-convoys/1942.html.

Offley, Ed. *The Burning Shore: How Hitler's U-Boats Brought World War II to America*. New York: Basic Books, 2014.

——. *Turning the Tide*. New York: Basic Books, 2011.

Padfield, Peter. *Dönitz: The Last Fuhrer*. London: Thistle Publishing, 2013.

Pitt, Barrie. *The Battle of the Atlantic*. Alexandria: Time-Life Books Inc., 1977.

Reminick, Gerald. *No Surrender: True Stories of the U.S. Navy Armed Guard in World War II*. Palo Alto: Glencannon Press, 2004.

Rohwer, Jürgen. *Axis Submarine Successes, 1939–1945*. Annapolis: US Naval Institute Press, 1983.

——. *The U-Boat Wars—1939-1945*. Annapolis: US Naval Institute Press, 1983.

Rust, Eric C. "The Case of Oskar Kusch and the Limits of U-boat Camaraderie in World War II: Reflections on a German Tragedy." International Journal of Naval History 1, No. 1, April 2002.

——. *U-Boat Commander Oskar Kusch: Anatomy of a Nazi-Era Betrayal and Judicial Murder*. Annapolis: US Naval Institute Press, 2020.

Sheffield, Gary. "The Battle of the Atlantic: The U-boat Peril." BBC website. Updated 03-30-2011. http://www.bbc.co.uk/history/worldwars/wwtwo/battle_atlantic_01.shtml.

Showall, Jak Malimann. *Hitler's Navy: A Reference Guide to the Kriegsmarine 1935-1945*. Seaworth Publishing, 2009.

——. *U-Boats Attack: The Battle of the Atlantic Witnessed by the Wolf Packs*. Gloucestershire: The History Press, 2011.

Snow, Richard. *A Measureless Peril*. Simon & Schuster, Inc., 2010.

Stern, Robert C. *U-Boats in Action*. Squadron/Signal Pub., 1977.

Symonds, Craig L. *World War II at Sea: A Global History*. New York: Oxford University Press, 2018.

Toye, Richard. *The Roar of the Lion: The Untold Story of Churchill's World War II Speeches*. Oxford University Press, Inc., 2013.

U-boat Aces website. "Battle of the Atlantic-America Joins the War." Accessed July 10, 2018. http://www.uboataces.com/boa-america.shtml.

White, David, and Daniel P. Murph, PhD. *The Everything World War II Book: North Africa*. Avon: Adams Media, 2007.

Williamson, Gordon. *U-Boat Tactics in World War II*. Botley and Oxford: Osprey Publishing Ltd., 2010.

Credits: Illustrations, Photographs, Charts, and Maps

Prologue

Figure 1. Artwork by Mark Gegenheimer, grandson of Ernest Bryan.

Figure 2. Uboat.net. https://www.uboat.net/men/.

Figure 3. Courtesy Bryan Family Collection.

Chapter One

Figure 4. National Archives and Records Administration, College Park, Maryland. Still Pictures, http://catalog.archives.gov/id/513512, Local Identifier: 44-PA-16.

Figure 5. National Archives and Records Administration, College Park, Maryland. Still Pictures, http://catalog.archives.gov/id/513543, Local Identifier: 44-PA-82.

Figure 6. National Archives and Records Administration, College Park, Maryland.

Figure 7. Illustration by the author.

Chapter Two

Figure 8. Courtesy Bryan Family Collection.

Figure 9. Courtesy Bryan Family Collection.

Chapter Three

Figure 10. Courtesy Bryan Family Collection.

Figure 11. Courtesy Bryan Family Collection.

Figure 12. Map by Tom Jonas.

Chapter Four

Figure 13. Courtesy Auke Visser, http://www.aukevisser.nl/inter-2/id186.htm.

Figure 14. Map by Tom Jonas.

Chapter Five

Figure 15. Map by Tom Jonas.

Figure 16. http://uboataces.com/uboat-type-vii.shtml

Chapter Six

Figure 17. http://www.uboataces.com/history-gallery.shtml

Figure 18. Map by Tom Jonas.

Chapter Seven

Figure 19. Courtesy Bryan Family Collection.

Figure 20. Courtesy Bryan Family Collection.

Chapter Eight

Figure 21. National Archives and Records Administration, College Park, Maryland.

Chapter Nine

Figure 22. Sketch by KptLt. Wilhelm Franken. National Archives and Records Administration, College Park, Maryland.

Figure 23. Map by Tom Jonas.

Figure 24. Courtesy State Library of New South Wales.

Figure 25. Courtesy Photoship. http://www.tynebuiltships.co.uk/S-Ships/sidibelabbes1949.html.

Chapter Eleven

Figure 26. Courtesy Auke Visser, http://www.aukevisser.nl/inter-2/id186.htm.

Figure 27. National Archives and Records Administration, College Park, Maryland.

Chapter Twelve

Figure 28. Courtesy Uwe Röttcher's Wilhelm Franken Collection.

Chapter Thirteen

Figure 29. Courtesy Uwe Röttcher's Wilhelm Franken Collection.

Figure 30. Courtesy Uwe Röttcher's Wilhelm Franken Collection.

Figure 31. German Wikipedia. https://commons.wikimedia.org/wiki/File:Nordfriedhof-Kiel-Grabmale-Erster-Weltkrieg.JPG.

Chapter Fourteen

Figure 32. Photograph by USAF Airman 2nd Class William J. Crouch. Courtesy Crouch Family Collection.

Figure 33. Photograph by USAF Airman 2nd Class William J. Crouch. Courtesy Crouch Family Collection.

Figure 34. Photograph by USAF Airman 2nd Class William J. Crouch. Courtesy Crouch Family Collection.

Figure 35. Illustration by the author.

Figure 36. Illustration by the author.

Epilogue

Figure 37. Courtesy Bryan Family Collection.

Figure 38. Courtesy Bryan Family Collection.

Figure 39. Courtesy Bryan Family Collection.

Figure 40. Courtesy Bryan Family Collection.

Appendix I

Figure 41. Courtesy Auke Visser, http://www.aukevisser.nl/inter-2/id186.htm

Figure 42. National Archives and Records Administration, College Park, Maryland.

Figure 43. National Archives and Records Administration, College Park, Maryland.

Appendix II

Figure 44. German U-boat. http://www.uboataces.com/uboat-type-vii.shtml.

Figure 45. National Archives and Records Administration, College Park, Maryland.

Appendix IV

Figure 46. German to English translation by Jerry Mason, http://www.uboatarchive.net.

Appendix V

Figure 47. Courtesy Bryan Family Collection.

ENDNOTES

Chapter 1 – America Enters World War II

1   Anthony McCarten, *Darkest Hour: How Churchill Brought England Back from the Brink* (New York: Harper Collins Publishers, 2017), 254-255.

2   Richard C. Hall, *Consumed by War: European Conflict in the 20th Century* (The University Press of Kentucky, 2010), 119-120, 158-159.

3   BBC, "President Roosevelt Proclaims Neutrality," *BBC News*, September 1, 1999. http://news.bbc.co.uk/2/hi/special_report/1999/08/99/world_war_ii/430187.stm.

4   "Fight Let's Go—Join the Navy" Poster, National Archives and Records Administration at College Park, Maryland – Still Pictures, Local Identifier: 44-PA-16. http://catalog.archives.gov/id/513512.

5   Richard Grunberger, *Germany 1918-1945* (London: B.T. Batsford Ltd., 1964), 165.

6   Ron Carlson, "The U.S. Navy Armed Guard." Accessed June 20, 2018. https://www.armed-guard.com/about-ag.html.

7   Naval History and Heritage Command, "1942: Atlantic Convoys." National Museum of the US Navy. Accessed September 9, 2018. https://www.history.navy.mil/content/history/museums/nmusn/explore/photography/wwii/wwii-atlantic/battle-of-the-atlantic/atlantic-convoys/1942.html.

8   Ed Offley, *The Burning Shore: How Hitler's U-Boats Brought World War II to America* (New York: Basic Books, 2014), 57-58.

9   Samuel E. Morison, *The Battle of the Atlantic 1939-1945*, Volume I (Boston: Little, Brown and Company, 1966), 126.

10   "Loose Lips Sink Ships" Poster, National Archives and Records Administration at College Park, Maryland – Still Pictures, Local Identifier: 44-PA-82. http://catalog.archives.gov/id/513543.

11   "Battle of the Atlantic-America Joins the War." Accessed July 10, 2018. http://www.uboataces.com/boa-america.shtml.

12   New England Historical Society, "U-Boat Attacks of World War II: 6 Months of Secret Terror in the Atlantic." Accessed August 20, 2017. http://newenglandhistoricalsociety.com/u-boat-attacks-of-world-war-ii.

13   Grunberger, *Germany 1918-1945*, 165.

14   Office of the Chief of Naval Operations, *History of the Armed Guard Afloat, World War II* (Washington Navy Yard, 1946), 1-15. Microfiche #173: United States Naval Administrative History of World War II, Navy Department Library.

15   Ibid.

16   Barrie Pitt, *The Battle of the Atlantic* (New York: Time-Life Books, Inc., 1977).

Chapter 3 – Ready to Serve His Country

17   William Hollenback, Foxboro, Massachusetts, US Navy Armed Guard veteran. Personal discussions with the author via phone conversations, 2017-2019.

18   Francis Kent, Hollywood, California, US Navy Armed Guard veteran. Personal discussions with the author via phone and email, 2012-2013.

19   Gregory Mackenzie, "US Navy Armed Guard Service in WW2." Ac-

cessed July 10, 2017. http://www.ahoy.tk-jk.net/macslog/USNavyArmed-GuardServicein.html.

20 Patrick Clancey and Otto Torriero, *Arming of Merchant Ships and Naval Armed Guard*, "Chapter II, The Men." Accessed July 10, 2017. https://www.ibiblio.org/hyperwar/USN/Admin-Hist/011-Convoy/index.html.

21 Patrick Clancey and Otto Torriero, *Armed Guard Afloat*, "Chapter IV, Battle of North Africa." Accessed August 17, 2017. https://www.ibiblio.org/hyperwar/USN/Admin-Hist/011-Convoy/index.html.

22 David White and Daniel P. Murph, PhD, *The Everything World War II Book: North Africa*, Chapter 5.

23 "Conduct of the War at Sea, An Essay by Admiral Karl Dönitz." Accessed July 12, 2018. https://www.history.navy.mil/research/library/online-reading-room/title-list-alphabetically/c/conduct-of-war-at-sea.html.

24 Winston Churchill, *The Second World War, Volume 2: Their Finest Hour*, "Chapter 30, Ocean Peril" (London: Cassell, 1949).

25 Patrick Clancey and Otto Torrier, *Armed Guard Afloat*, "Chapter III, Battle of the Atlantic." Accessed August 30, 2018. https://www.ibiblio.org/hyperwar/USN/Admin-Hist/011-Convoy/index.html.

26 Ibid.

27 Russell Corder, "WWII, Hazardous Duty with the Naval Armed Guard." Accessed October 17, 2018. https://warfarehistorynetwork.com/daily/wwii/hazardous-duty-with-the-naval-armed-guard/.

Chapter 4 – Convoy UGS-4: *Esso Montpelier*

28 Gerald Reminick, *No Surrender* (Palo Alto, California: Glencannon Press, 2004), 5.

29 Morison, *The Battle of the Atlantic*, 211-212.

30 John Bunker, *Liberty Ships: The Ugly Ducklings of WWII* (Salem, New

Hampshire: Ayer Company Publishers, Inc., 1972), 81-111.

31 Seaman 1/c Ernest Bryan, personal journals and family album.

32 Lt. James Thornhill, Armed Guard Commanding Officer of the SS *Esso Montpelier,* Voyage Report, National Archives and Records Administration at College Park, Maryland.

33 Gudmundur Helgason, *All Convoys Hit by U-boats.* Accessed October 20, 2017. http://uboat.net/ops/convoys/convoys.php?convoy=UGS-4.

34 Ibid.

35 Ibid.

Chapter 5 – Early years, Wilhelm Franken in Germany and at War

36 History.com editors, "Adolf Hitler is named chancellor of Germany," History, October 28, 2009. Accessed August 2019. https://www.history.com/this-day-in-history/adolf-hitler-is-named-chancellor-of-germany.

37 Jurgen Rohwer, *Axis Submarine Successes 1939-1945* (Annapolis: Naval Institute Press, 1983), 227.

38 Helgason, "24th Flotilla." Accessed July 10, 2020. https://uboat.net/flotillas/24flo.htm.

39 "German Type VIIC U-Boat." Accessed August 10, 2020. http://uboataces.com/uboat-type-vii.shtml.

40 The High Command of the German Navy, *The U-Boat Commander's Handbook* (Gettysburg: Thomas Publications, October 1989), Section I, 17-39.

41 Ibid., Sections III-VII.

42 Helgason, "Ships Hit by U-boats, *Kirkland.*" Accessed July 15, 2020. https://uboat.net/allies/merchants/ship/1563.html.

Chapter 6– Evasive Measures...Crash Dive

43 Jurgen Rohwer, *Axis Submarine Successes of World War II* (Annapolis: Naval Institute Press, 1999), 235.

44 Andrew Lycet, "Breaking Germany's Enigma Code," *BBC History.* Updated 2011-02-17. http://www.bbc.co.uk/history/worldwars/wwtwo/enigma_01.shtml.

45 Jak Showell, *U-Boats Attack!: The Battle of the Atlantic Witnessed by the Wolf Packs* (London: The History Press, 2011), 160.

46 *German U-boat War Diaries* (*Kriegstagebuch U565*), Secret Command Document (1943), Microfilm. Records of the Chief of Naval Operations, Group 38, boxes 136 and 137. National Archives and Records Administration at College Park, Maryland.

47 Helgason, "Ships Hit by U-boats, *Nathanael Greene.*" Accessed January 10, 2020. http://www.uboat.net/allies/merchants/.

48 Helgason, "The Men of the U-Boats." Accessed January 10, 2020. https://www.uboat.net/men/.

49 Helgason, "Allies." Accessed January 10, 2020. http://www.uboat.net/allies/.

Chapter 7 – Times of Courage

50 *Navy Department General Instructions for Commanding Officers of Naval Armed Guards on Merchant Ships*, "Chapter III. After Sailing, Section 1. At Sea," 41-42. Accessed March 10, 2020. https://www.ibiblio.org/hyperwar/USN/ref/NAG/NAG-3.html.

51 Ernest Bryan, personal letters from family album.

52 Wilhelm Franken, personal letters provided by Uwe Röttcher, Hannover-Langenhagen, Germany, 2016-2017.

Chapter 8 – Convoy UGS-7 Underway

53 Arnold Hague, *The Allied Convoy System 1939-1945: Its Organization, Defence, and Operation*, UGS Convoy Series (Annapolis: US Naval Institute Press, 2000). Accessed March 30, 2020. http://www.convoyweb.org.uk/ugs/index.html.

54 Helgason, "U-Boat Operations." Accessed September 10, 2017. https://www.uboat.net/ops/.

55 Helgason, "Allies" and "Ships Hit by U-Boats, *James W. Denver*." Accessed September 10, 2017. https://www.uboat.net/allies/merchants/crews/ship2865.html.

56 John Gorley Bunker, "Battle of the Atlantic," *Liberty Ships: The Ugly Ducklings of World War II*, 1972. Accessed October 10, 2019. https://www.armed-guard.com/ag77.html.

57 Frank C. Walker, Postmaster General of the US, "United States at War, December 7, 1942 | December 7, 1943," *Army and Navy Journal*. Accessed October 15, 2019. https://igreenbaum.com/2012/04/02/wartime-postmaster-details-the-work-of-mail-delivery-in-wwii/.

58 "Ship Log for US Ship *Foote* (DD511) 9 April, 1943, Half-masted colors at 1530," Ship Log for USS *Charles Ausburne*, National Archives and Records Administration at College Park, Maryland.

59 James Holland, *Fortress Malta: An Island Under Siege, 1940–1943* (London: Miramax Books, 2003), 417.

60 Naval History and Heritage Command, "Wartime Instructions for United States Merchant Vessels, United States Fleet, Headquarters of the Commander-In-Chief, 1942." Accessed November 30, 2019. https://www.history.navy.mil/research/library/online-reading-room/title-list-alphabetically/w/wartime-instructions-united-states-merchant-vessels-1942.html.

Chapter 10 – Delivering the Vital Cargo

61 Lengel, Edward G., "The Rock of Legend: Gibraltar," *Military History*

Quarterly, July 2014. Accessed August 20, 2020. https://www.historynet.com/rock-legend-gibraltar.htm.

62 United States Holocaust Memorial Museum, "Tunisia Campaign." Accessed November 7, 2020. https://encyclopedia.ushmm.org/content/en/article/tunisia-campaign.

63 "Italian auxiliary ship *Olterra*." Accessed March 20, 2019. https://infogalactic.com/w/index.php?title=Italian_auxiliary_ship_Olterra&oldid=709623238.

64 *Esso Montpelier*, "Port Attack Bonus." Accessed March 30, 2019. http://www.aukevisser.nl/inter-2/id1215.htm.

Chapter 11 – Homeward Bound

65 Ibid.

66 William Hollenback, Massachusetts, Navy Armed Guard veteran Personal discussions with the author via personal phone conversations 2017-2019.

67 Dr Gary Sheffield, "The Battle of the Atlantic: The U-boat peril." Updated 03-30-2011. http://www.bbc.co.uk/history/worldwars/wwtwo/battle_atlantic_01.shtml.

Chapter 12 – Defeat of the U-Boats

68 The High Command of the German Navy, *The U-Boat Commanders' Handbook* (Gettysburg: Thomas Publications, October 1989), Section II, 60.

69 Naval History and Heritage Command, *German Navy U-Boat (Submarine) Headquarters War Logs, World War II* in the Collection of the US Navy Department Library. Accessed August 20, 2020. https://www.history.navy.mil/research/library/research-guides/german-navy-u-boat-submarine-headquarters-war-logs-from-world-war-ii.html.

70   Clay Blair, *Hitler's U-boat War: Vol. II, The Hunted, 1942–1945* (New York: Random House, 1998), 210.

71   David Miller, *U-Boats: The Illustrated History of the Raiders of the Deep* (Washington: Brassey's, Inc., 2000), 126.

72   Robert C. Stern, *U-Boats in Action* (Squadron/Signal Publication, 1977). Accessed July 15, 2018. https://en.wikipedia.org/wiki/Black_May_ (1943).

73   Dönitz, *The Conduct of the War at Sea, An Essay*, 23.

74   Personal letters written by Wilhelm Franken, *U-565*, dated March 4, 1943. Courtesy of Uwe Röttcher. Personal collection from Friedel Schlimme, *U-565* crewmember. Email 11/21/2017 from Uwe Röttcher, Hannover, Langenhagen, Germany, to author.

Chapter 13 – The Tragic Loss of a Hero

75   Ibid.

76   Ibid.

77   Blair, *Hitler's U-boat War: Vol. II*, 461.

78   Eric C. Rust, *U-Boat Commander Oskar Kusch: Anatomy of a Nazi-Era Betrayal and Judicial Murder* (Annapolis: Naval Institute Press, 2020), 179-81.

79   Eric C. Rust, "The Case of Oskar Kusch and the Limits of U-Boat Camaraderie in World War II: Reflections on a German Tragedy," *International Journal of Naval History*, Volume 1, no. 1, April 2002. http://www. ijnhonline.org/issues/volume-1-2002/apr-2002-vol-1-issue-1.

80   Blair, *Hitler's U-boat War: Vol. II*, 526.

81   "The U-Boats, *U-565*." Accessed October 20, 2017. https://www. uboat.net/boats/.

82   From shared personal files of Uwe Röttcher.

83   Helmut Jacksch, *U 565: Das Boot Und Seine Menschen* (*U 565: The Boat and Its People*), publisher: self-pub., nd.

84   Rainer Busch and Hans-Joachim Röll, *German U–boat Commanders of World War II* (London: Greenhill Books, 1999).

85   Personal letters written by Wilhelm Franken, *U-565*. Courtesy of Uwe Röttcher. Personal collection from Friedel Schlimme, *U-565* crew-member. Email 11/21/2017 from Uwe Röttcher, Hannover, Langenhagen, Germany, to author.

86   Translation from German by Eric C. Rust, PhD.

Chapter 14 – War Comes to an End

87   Wikipedia contributors, "Tehran Conference." Accessed September 3, 2019. https://en.wikipedia.org/w/index.php?title=Tehran_Conference&oldid=902205105.

88   "Milestones: 1937–1945," Office of the Historian, US Department of State. Retrieved September 3, 2019.

89   "Battle of the Bulge." Updated July 22, 2020. https://www.history.com/topics/world-war-ii/battle-of-the-bulge.

90   Peter Padfield, *Dönitz: The Last Fuhrer* (London: Thistle Publishing, 2013), 462-463.

91   "The U-Boats: Revised Fates." Accessed October 15, 2019. https://uboat.net/fates/revised.html.

92   Winston Churchill, "Telegram from Prime Minister Winston Churchill to US President Truman June 1945," Catalogue ref: PREM 3/413/7, 10-11. Accessed March 30, 2020. https://www.nationalarchives.gov.uk/education/worldwar2/theatre-assets/atlantic/pdf/a-battle-of-the-atlantic.pdf.

93   Ibid.

94   Naval History and Heritage Command, "US Navy Personnel in World War II: Service and Casualty Statistics." Updated February 27, 2017. https://www.history.navy.mil/research/library/online-reading-room/title-list-alphabetically/u/us-navy-personnel-in-world-war-ii-service-and-casualty-statistics.html

95   "American Merchant Marine at War." Updated June 24, 2019. www.usmm.org/ww2.html.

96   Naval Historical Society of Australia, "British and German Submarine Statistics of World War II." Accessed October 15, 2019. https://www.navy-history.org.au/british-and-german-submarine-statistics-of-world-war-ii/.

97   Ron Carlson, "World War II U.S. Navy Armed Guard and U.S. Merchant Marine." Accessed September 19, 2019. https://www.armed-guard.com/about-ag.html.

INDEX

A

Abel, Ulrich 134
aircraft 37, 39, 127
Algiers, Algeria
   shore leave in 104
   surrender of 31
   UGS-7 destination 88, 96, 97
Allies. See also specific operation or campaign
Allies
   Casablanca Conference 37
   Tehran Conference 142
   term defined 11
   turning points for 75, 115, 126
American Shooting Season (Happy Times) 11
anti-submarine weapons, technology 39, 56
Arctic convoys 119
Armed Guard . See Navy Armed Guard (U.S.)
Arnold, Henry H. \ 144
Athenia 6, 43
Athens, Greece 132
atomic bomb 146
Axis . See also specific operation or campaign
   North Africa surrender 108, 115
   term defined 11

B

Barham 51
Battle of Britain 9
Battle of the Atlantic . See also *U-565*; U-boat campaigns; UGS-4 convoy; UGS-7 convoy
   Axis defeat 126, 135
   Churchill on 145
   dangers of 119
   description 6, 38
   German U-boat withdrawal 115

Battle of the Bulge 144
Bitter, Georg von 136
Black May 127
Bletchley Park 57
Bryan, Enoch (father) 20, 73
Bryan, Enoch, Jr. (brother)
   military service 26, 154
   photo of 155
Bryan, Ernest
   in Algiers 104
   awards received 157
   bar fights 106
   burial place photo 159
   childhood 20
   childhood home 23
   civilian positions 157
   death 157
   fears of 40, 46, 70, 79
   first active duty 33, 39
   letter to father 73
   marriage and children 23, 34, 70, 154, 157, 158
   naval assignment 30
   Navy enlistment, training 26
   photos of 3, 20, 27, 28, 70, 71, 155, 156, 157
   post-war military service 154
   rating exam 81, 112, 115
   Sidi-Bel-Abbes sinking and 3, 96, 118
   stress in 104, 105
   UGS-7 journal entries 79, 80, 95, 113, 187
Bryan, Gretchen (daughter) 156
Bryan, Linda (daughter) . See Dunn, Linda Dawn
Bryan, Michael (son) 155
Bryan, Paul (brother)
   military service 26, 154
   photo of 155
Bryan, Sharon (daughter) 154
Bryan, Tempa Hires (mother) 20

Bryan, Vera McDaniel (wife)
  burial place photo 159
  death 158
  in New York with Ernest 70
  marriage to Ernest 23, 157
  photos of 70, 157
  visionary dream 1, 114

C

Camerata 109
Casablanca Conference 37
Casablanca, Morocco 31
casualty figures 148, 149
Charles C. Pinckney 42, 43, 45
China, casualties 148
Churchill, Winston
  Casablanca Conference 37
  on Battle of the Bulge; Battle of the
  Bulge 144
  on merchant marine; merchant
  marine 151
  on U-boat threat; U-boat threat
  32, 120
  plead for U.S. support 8
  prime ministership 8
  Tehran Conference 142
  telegrams to Truman 145, 148
City of Flint 42
Clark, Mark W. 144
Clyde, Scotland 117
convoy systems . See also specific
convoys or ships
  convoy routing 203
  photo, illus. 16, 17, 87
  tactics 60
  types and formations 17
Crowder, Lionel E. 83, 87
Cyclops 12

D

Daressalem 136
D-Day (Operation Overlord) 143
Dönitz, Karl
  Allied losses to 15

Black May 127
cease-fire order 145
convoy system effect on 17
Franken service under 50
Kusch court-martial and 134
Operation Drumbeat 11
promotion 31
draft recruitment poster 10
Dunn, Linda Dawn 23, 71, 158

E

Eisenhower, Dwight D.
  D-Day 143
  photos of 143, 144
Enigma machine 57
Enola Gay 146
Esso Montpelier See also HX-242
convoy; UGS-4 convoy; UGS-7 convoy
  in Algiers 104
  Armed Guard personnel 164
  battle protocol 72
  Bryan first convoy 39
  cargo 37
  in Gibraltar 59
  guns aboard 42, 165
  number of voyages 119
  photos of 36, 113, 161
  ship food 107
  trade route 36, 41
  U-565 encounter 93, 94, 119
Eureka (Tehran Conference) 142

F

Firth of Clyde 117
France 128, 143
Franken, Hector August (father) 48
Franken, Waltraut Schomburg (wife)
53, 132, 134, 137
Franken, Wilhelm See also *U-565*
  as staff officer 132, 136
  awards received 51, 123, 124
  burial place photos 139
  childhood 48
  commendation from Italy 123

crew's esteem for 132, 137
death 136
early career 51
first U-boat command 51
journal entries 129, 132
at Kiel University 48, 49
marriage and children 54, 132, 134, 137, 140
navy training 50
newspaper article 124, 125
personal letter 75
photos of 2, 127
promise to crew 132, 133
seventh patrol log 59, 60, 67
source material 159
war diary and FdU, BdU comments 167, 199
war diary patrol report 177
Friedeburg, Hans-Georg von 134

G

Germany . See also U-boat campaigns; specific battles
casualties 148, 149
defeat in Europe 145
Operation Weserübung 7
thousand-bomber raid 54
war declared on U.S. 10
war diary comments 167, 169
Gibraltar 59, 105
Glasgow, Scotland 117
Godt, Eberhard 134
Great Britain . See Battle of Britain; Churchill, Winston; RAF
Great Depression 21, 24, 48
Greer 9

H

Haitian Coast Guard 157
Happy Times (American Shooting Season) 11
hedgehogs 39
Hiroshima, Japan 146
Hitler, Adolph . See also Germany

assassination attempt 135
influence of 49
U-boats and 31, 127
Hollenback, William
biographical sketch 159
convoys 115, 119
enlistment 28
memories and healing 158
on shore leave 106
Sidi-Bel-Abbes sinking and 96
on U-535 encounter 119
human torpedoes 108
HX-242 convoy
destinations 116
fleet list 191
iceberg threat 116, 117, 118
Middleton log report 116
route map 116

I

Instrument of Surrender (Japan) 147
Iron Cross award 51
Italy
Franken commendation 123
human torpedoes 108
war diary comments 167, 169, 199

J

Jacksch, Helmut 136
James W. Denver 79
Japan
bombing and surrender 146
casualties 148
John A. Brown 117
Julia Ward Howe 42, 46

K

Kent, Francis 29, 30
Kiel, Germany 48, 49
Kiel War Cemetery photos 139
Kirkland 53, 62
Knight's Cross award 123, 124, 136
Kreisch, Leo 124
Kusch, Oskar-Heinz 133

L

La Spezia, Italy 53, 56, 58, 67
letter writing 80
Loose Lips Sink Ships campaign 14,
15, 79
Lüdden, Siegfried 136

M

Mahsud 109
Malta 83, 115
McDaniel, Vera . See Bryan, Vera
McDaniel
merchant marine
    battle protocol 71
    Churchill recognition 151
    civilian volunteers 7
    ships lost 149, 150
    U.S. personnel, casualties 149
Michigan 93, 98
Middleton, Elwyn
    HX-242 log report 116
    UGS-7 log report 84, 99, 114
Mürwik Naval School 50

N

Nagasaki, Japan 146
Nathanael Greene attack
    Allies' report 62
    Franken report 59
    map of attack 62
National Defense Medal of U.S. 157
National Memorial Cemetery of
Arizona 159
Navy Armed Guard (U.S.)
    casualties 150
    convoy systems 16, 17
    description 29
    fears and dangers of 40
    mission and dutiesmission and
    duties 33, 84
    mottos 30
    as Navy stepchild 73, 155
    personnel 148, 164
    reestablishment 15

ship living conditions 33, 81, 107
    training schools 28
    as unsung heroes 150
Nicaina 117
Normandy, France 143
North Africa campaign . See also
UGS-7 convoy
    Axis surrender, defeat 108, 115,
    126
    Operation Torch 30
    ULTRA role in 57
Norwegian Campaign 7

O

Olterra 108
Operation Drumbeat 12
Operation Neuland 13
Operation Overlord (D-Day) 143
Operation Paukenschlag. See
Operation Drumbeat
Operation Torch 30, 106
Operation Valkyrie 135
Operation Weserübung 7
Oran, Algeria
    Nathanael Greene near 62, 64
    surrender of 31
    UGS-4 destination 41
    UGS-7 destination 95
    UGS-7 near 92

P

P-38 fighter planes 37
Partridge 56, 62
Pat Harrison 108, 109
Patton, George S. 144
Pearl Harbor attack 10, 13, 26
Port au Prince, Haiti 157
Pula, Croatia 128

R

RAF (Royal Air Force) 9, 54
Reuben James 9
Rommel, Erwin 83, 108
Roosevelt, Franklin D.

Casablanca Conference 37
death 145
neutrality 9
photos of 143, 144
Tehran Conference 142
Royal Air Force (RAF) 9, 54
Royal Navy 6

S

Salamis, Greece 53, 133
Schomburg, Waltraut . See Franken,
Waltraut Schomburg
Seminole 62, 64
Sidi-Bel-Abbes
photo of 99
sinking of 2, 93, 94, 95, 97, 118
Vera's visionary dream 1, 114
Siege of Malta 83
Soviet Union
casualties 148
Tehran Conference 142
war declared on Japan 146
Stalin, Joseph 142
Straits of Gibraltar 78, 105

T

Tehran Conference 142
Thornhill, James 41, 46
thousand-bomber raid 54
Toulon, France 128
Truman, Harry S.
Presidency 145
telegrams from Churchill 145, 148
Tunisia 126

U

U-30 6
U-154 commander 133
U-565
BdU recognition 67
boat type 51, 56
end of 135
Esso Montpelier encounter 93, 94,
119

Franken's last patrols 128
intercepted radio traffic 178
Kirkland sinking 53
map of ship attacks 62
missed targets 122
Nathanael Greene attack 59
Partridge sinking 56
photos of 56, 167
Seminole attack 64
total Allied cargo destroyed 123
UGS-7 attack 2, 90, 94
war diary and FdU, BdU comments
167, 199
U-boat campaigns
casualties 149
cease-fire order 145
Churchill on 32, 120
defeat in Atlantic 126, 135
Dönitz campaigns 12, 15, 17, 31
tactics 51
U-boat Commander's Handbook 51
UG convoys, described 36
UGS-4 convoy
battle alarms 101
fleet list 37, 162
route map 41
voyage details 41
UGS-7 convoy
attack of 2, 90, 94
Bryan journal entries 79, 80, 95,
113, 187
departure and route 78
first ship lost 79
fleet list 171
in Gibraltar; Gibraltar 105
Middleton log report 84, 99, 114
return voyage 112
route map 97
ULTRA intelligence 57, 75, 127
United Nations proposal 142
United States . See also Navy Armed
Guard (U.S.)
casualties 148, 149
coastal U-boat attacks on 12, 15,
17

    draft recruitment poster 10
    military personnel 148, 164
    Navy unpreparedness 13
    neutrality 9
    shipbuilding 18, 38
    war declared 10

V

V-E Day 145

W

War Shipping Administration (WSA) 36
weather 40, 42, 81, 113
World War I 15, 105
World War II . See also specific battles, campaigns, or countries
    beginnings 6
    casualties 148
    end of 146
    global powers in 11
    V-E Day 145

About the Author

Lee Bryan grew up in military family life while traveling throughout the United States and other countries. Her travels resulted in exposure to multiple cultures and environments. After obtaining her degree in business, Bryan's work career began in the technology industry, where she held various management positions and again traveled broadly in the United States and internationally. She retired after a twenty-five-year track record of success in the corporate world and currently lives in Arizona with her husband Bill, enjoying her passions as a photographer and genealogy researcher, as well as discovering and documenting family history. Bryan serves as a board member for the Disabled Artists Foundation and holds a certificate in Life Coaching. Currently, she is also pursuing a Master of Arts degree in World War II Studies.